FIGURE IT OUT
WHEN YOU
GET THERE

FIGURE IT OUT
WHEN YOU
GET THERE

A Memoir of Stories About Living Life First and
Watching How Everything Else Falls In Line

BARAK HULLMAN

Published by Pike & Vagenheim

Stay updated about new books and speaking engagements at **www.barakhullman.com**

Cover design by Emir Paja
Typeset by Euan Monaghan
Photo of author by Roni Isaiah

ISBN: 978-0-9993896-0-7

Write about what you know.

— Mark Twain

To my wife Noga and our children Alma, Aidel, Shuvi, Natan Chaim, Avigail, Eliana and Levi Yitzchak (may they live long) for giving me the quiet and peace of mind to write this book.

Even though they didn't.

— Barak Hullman

CONTENTS

MUFFIN TOPS

I first started writing this book as a philosophy of life using personal stories to help explain the ideas. When I showed my wife the first chapter she told me, "Honestly, the stories are much more interesting. Why don't you just write a book of personal stories?"

It reminded me of a Seinfeld episode where one of the characters opens a bakery that just sells the tops of muffins, since that's the part that everyone likes best.

This is a book of muffin tops.

Plant and water a watermelon seed and under the right circumstances you'll get a watermelon. Each watermelon will taste and look different. Plant and water me and you'll get a very Jewish book.

There's a glossary of Hebrew/Yiddish terms in the back.

SOMETIMES I'VE WANTED TO THANK THAT IDIOTIC KID

The Boy Scouts saved my life. I was such a poor student in school that, without the validation I got from the Boy Scouts, I don't know where I would have ended up. I didn't have the mental energy to "apply myself" as the adults in my life liked to say. But the Boy Scouts was full of adventure, challenges, respect, honor, freedom, independence, and a chance to use all of my God-given talents. Within a few months of joining, I was made a patrol leader. I barely understood how the Scouts worked when I started leading a group of ten boys at thirteen years old, but it was what I needed. It was like a really strong cup of coffee when you've been sleeping for so long you can't seem to wake up.

I flew through the ranks and quickly became the "Senior Patrol Leader." This meant I was effectively running the entire troop of thirty-plus boys. I was fifteen years old; the youngest Senior Patrol Leader in the troop's history. The boys looked up to me. They phoned me at home. They confided in me. They asked me questions about how to deal with their parents' divorce or the bully in school. I went from a bored kid with no direction to a young man with purpose and a fire in his heart. I'm still that young man, just physically older and with a bigger fire than back then. I thank God every day for the Boy Scouts.

The Order of the Arrow is like the Honor Society of the Boy Scouts. You can only be admitted by troop nomination. Then you need to do additional volunteer work in your community. Afterwards, you go through what we called "The Ordeal." It lasted for two days. You fasted during the day, as you worked fixing roofs in the local national park and slept in the woods with no tent or sleeping bag. There was no talking during the daytime and we had a big feast at the end of the work day.

A year after being admitted to the Order of the Arrow, I became one of the leaders in my chapter. This ratcheted-up the community volunteering. The usual was fixing rundown buildings in public institutions or volunteering in a soup kitchen or a homeless shelter. A good friend of mine at the time had a dream to start a Boy Scout troop in the poorest, most violent part of downtown Miami; Overtown it was called. Would I help?

"No way!" was my first answer. "I'm not going to get myself killed over a Boy Scout troop." He told me that starting the troop would be enough to get the leadership position that I wanted in the Order of the Arrow (he was the head of the committee that decided on the leadership positions; if he recommended me, I was in) and that we would do it in the Baptist Church, which was a safe haven in the neighborhood. He'd already done the groundwork. Everything was ready. He just needed someone motivated like me to start the troop. He promised to drive me there himself and, if anything ever happened, I was free to never return again.

I agreed and the next week we drove into Overtown in my friend's car, an old Mustang without seatbelts. I joked with him that I wasn't sure what was more dangerous: driving in his car or going into Overtown. I grew up in South Florida. I had driven past Overtown a hundred times on my way to work at my father's eyeglass store on Miami Beach but I never got off on the Overtown exit until now.

The sun had set as we were driving down South. We turned off in darkness, right into the worst neighborhood in Miami.

Overtown spelled riots, shootings, open drug use and prostitutes selling their wares. I had mentally prepared myself for what I might see, but it was worse than I had imagined. We stopped at the first light and several people came over to us. Of course, we didn't open the window, but one tried to sell us drugs and another was a prostitute.

The traffic lights changed and we kept driving until we reached the Baptist Church; a modest building with a white picket fence and a trim lawn.

From the parking lot, we walked into the church without a problem. The church choir was practicing in the main church and we were in a back room. The boys were waiting for us; I was in charge. My friend said if I needed anything he'd be in the church office. I introduced myself and started working my Boy Scout magic. Within a few months the boys were really shaping up. I was elected to the leadership position I was working toward.

The Order of the Arrow was based on Native American traditions. We wore full Native American clothes with headdresses, shoes, warpaint; the works. The headdresses were provided for us; the rest we had to buy or make ourselves. Only a few of the "brothers" were allowed to wear these costumes. There were ceremonies related to the Order of the Arrow and a book with entire speeches to memorize for each ceremony.

As a leader of the chapter, I played the part of an ancient Native American elder during the induction ceremony for new brothers into the Order of the Arrow. It was a beautiful ceremony. The costume was authentic and impressive.

We were in the heart of the forest. Leading up to the area where

I began my speech was a path lit up with little fires in tin cans. Each had a roll of toilet paper soaked in some type of flammable liquid. Behind me was a large bonfire that I had lit.

I was given a five gallon plastic jug of gasoline and a cup to top up the tin cans. I was told "always use the cup." Got it. Always use the cup. I had a few groups of inductees come and go to my station already. I checked the book to make sure I wasn't forgetting any lines from my speech. Then I fed the bonfire and walked with the jug of gasoline to check the tin can fires. Some of them were running low. I poured the gas into the cup and then into the tin can. But this seemed so inefficient. Why bother with the cup when I could just pour the gasoline directly from the jug? I quickly learned why.

As I was pouring the gasoline from the five gallon jug, the fire jumped from the tin can up the stream of gasoline and the jug exploded. The gas was all over my body and I was on fire. There was no one around. We had picked this remote location so that no one could even see the bonfire. The new inductees were brought blindfolded until they reached the fire-lit path.

When I was a kid, I spent a lot of time watching TV. There were commercials from Smokey the Bear in which he would say, "Only you can prevent forest fires." Oy vey, Smokey. I really blew that one. Then I remembered this commercial I'd seen over and over. If you catch on fire, "Stop, drop and roll." At last, TV had done me some good. Within a split second of catching on fire, I stopped, dropped and rolled and, it turns out, it works! I had a sunburn, but nothing more. I quickly took off my burned clothes and stamped on them. Fortunately I still had on my shorts and a t-shirt that I'd been wearing under the Native American costume. I was fine, thank God, but now I had another problem; a raging forest fire that I had started and no one there to help me put it out.

We were in a Boy Scout camp, a tract of forest bought by the Boy Scouts a hundred years before. I knew there were other troops camping out there. Realizing the severity of the fire, I ran faster than I had ever run in my life on the dirt roads until I found a troop. I ran into their campground and explained as quickly as possible to the Scoutmaster what had happened. He couldn't believe it. I showed him the fire in the distance. Then he sprung into action. He called the whole troop together, maybe forty boys, and told them, "We're going to put out that forest fire."

We ran back to where the fire was. My spot was above a lake with a beautiful view. We grabbed buckets and made an assembly line from the lake to the fire. I was the deepest in the lake filling up the buckets with water. We would send bucket after bucket up the hill to the fire. In the meantime the fire department had been called, but they were about fifteen minutes away. My biceps were spent pulling up buckets of water from the lake. My arms were quivering from exhaustion, but only death would have stopped me sending water up the line.

Eventually the fire was put out. It was a massive fire. This was summertime in Miami, in a tinder-dry forest, acres of which were consumed. The camp ranger asked me what happened. I told him the truth and he freaked out, "Didn't anyone tell you to use the cup?"

Ten years or so later, I went back to the forest. I went on my own, not with any Scout troop or for any organized event. I tried to find the part that I had burned down, but I couldn't. There was a new camp ranger at the time. I went to his house and told him I was there the night the huge forest fire happened and could he please tell me where the burned part of the forest was. He looked at me like a police detective.

It seemed like he was about to say to me, "Are you the kid that burned it down?" but he didn't. He said the burned part of the forest had grown back already and, "Whoever burned it down actually did us a big favor." It had been an old part of the forest and many of the trees were dead. The fire had burned down a lot of the old, dead trees and now it's the most beautiful part of the forest. "Sometimes I've wanted to thank that idiotic kid for what he did," the camp ranger said to me, and then he changed his mind. "No, if I ever met him, I'd tell him what an idiot he was."

KING DAVID'S
DIRECT DESCENDENT

A lot of the beggars of Jerusalem know me because I treat them with respect. Some of them know me by name and know a little bit about me. Some know where I live. Some have my phone number. I try to help as many people as I can without endangering myself or my family. The beggars of Jerusalem are pretty harmless anyway.

There was one beggar whose name was David. He was originally from the Southwest of America and had somehow or another ended up in Jerusalem. He lived in a cave in the Jerusalem forest full of water bottles and personal items. David said he was preparing for the end of the world.

He used to play a little drum and sing a tune while collecting money on the street. A lot of the beggars I know just ask for money, but he made an effort. He would sing, "*Daveed melech yisrael chai, chai v'kayam*" (King David of the Jewish people lives, lives forever).

Every time I saw him I gave him a few coins and asked him how he was doing. He always had the same answer, "I'm gonna make it. I'm gonna make it." Then he would pull out some papers with thoughts he wrote down. They made no sense to me at all. He was obsessed with showing his direct lineage to King David. Sometimes he thought he was King David reincarnated.

I thought to myself, sure, he's crazy and lives in a cave, of course he thinks he's gonna "make it." Make what exactly? Was this called "making it?" Time and again I would come across David on the street and we'd have the same conversation.

I've had a lot of hard times in my adult life and, when I would hear David saying he was going to make it, I would think, if *he's* gonna make it, then for sure *I'm* gonna make it. I even started using his phrase. People would ask me how I'm doing and I'd tell them "I'm gonna make it." This phrase often gave me strength in my hardest of times. I repeated it to myself over and over again "I'm gonna make it. I'm gonna make it."

David was in and out of homeless shelters, kind people's homes, prison and the hospital, and then back on the streets again. Sometimes David was around and other times you wouldn't see him for weeks or even months.

One day I asked a friend of mine who knew David well where he was. "He didn't make it," was his answer.

"What?" I asked. "He died?"

"Yep," my friend said, "he didn't make it."

Or maybe he did. After all, what are we all here for? You have this success or the other, but we all leave this world eventually. We're just leaves, piled on top of older leaves making up the ground for the next generation to walk on.

David left a legacy, at least with me. He didn't have a family or a home, but he had an optimistic message for anyone who was willing to stop and listen to him. Thanks to David, I have found the strength to continue when it seems like all life has given me are dead ends. I just keep repeating to myself, "I'm gonna make it. I'm gonna make it." And eventually I do.

GET ON A PLANE AND NEVER COME BACK HERE AGAIN

One of my closest friends from Jerusalem was getting married in New York at the age of forty-six. It was his first time getting married. I told him years before that when he got married, if I could afford it, I would fly in from Jerusalem for the wedding. My business had done better than usual and, with my wife's permission, I booked flights to visit my family in South Florida and then to go to my friend's wedding in New York. He was getting married on a Sunday. We spent *Shabbos* (the Jewish Sabbath) together in Crown Heights, Brooklyn.

Sunday morning we went to *daven* (pray) at 770 Eastern Parkway, Chabad International Headquarters. It's a *minyan* (prayer quorum) factory there. Every few minutes a new *minyan* was starting. We found a *minyan* to *daven* with. I had quite a few things in my *tallis* bag and, since it was the month of Elul, I also had my shofar (a ram's horn used as a musical instrument). I had packed the shofar at the top of the bag so it wouldn't knock into anything when I was travelling.

This was the shofar that my parents gave me when I was thirteen, at my Bar *Mitzvah*. I used to blow the shofar in our synagogue for Rosh Hashanah (the Jewish New Year). It was a beautiful shofar with a great sound. I started playing the French Horn when I was thirteen and all of those years of practice made playing the shofar feel like a piece of cake. Over the years I blew the shofar during the Rosh Hashanah services and always got compliments, which led to people wanting to see my shofar. The shofar itself also got compliments.

After I finished *davening* at the *minyan* at 770, I noticed my friend was deep in prayer. It was his wedding day. He'd waited a long time to get married, having friends that were already grandparents at his age. This was a big day for him and he wanted to thank God for it through prayer. I understood that and occupied myself with learning Torah. We left 770 half an hour later.

We had a whole schedule planned for the morning. We quickly packed our things and left. By two o'clock we were at the wedding hall, four hours early. I saw my friend was well taken care of and I went outside for a little walk. I had over three hours left until the wedding began. No one was taking pictures of me.

The wedding was in the heart of the American Chassidic community in Williamsburg. Even though I had lived in New Jersey for several years before moving to Israel, I had never been to Williamsburg. Besides seeing my aging grandparents, visiting Chassidic Williamsburg was the highlight of my trip.

It was a little shocking. I'm used to being around a lot of Jews—I live in Jerusalem, after all—but not in Brooklyn. I'd never seen anything like this, even in Mea Shearim. All of the store signs were in Yiddish. The men were dressed in black, the women with their *sheitels* (wigs) and strollers. I loved all of this Jewish energy. I felt that, after a week in the States and feeling out of place as a Jew, I was finally amongst my people.

But I wasn't. I don't speak Yiddish. I speak Hebrew and English. I know a few phrases in Yiddish, but I'm not Haredi. So, as much as I loved seeing all of these Jews, they didn't seem to love me back so much. I stood out like a red balloon amongst a stadium of black balloons, but I didn't really care.

I walked around like I was in Disneyland. I passed by a row of school buses filled with little Yiddish-speaking kids with their checkered shirts and *peyos* (sidelocks). I was so excited to see these kids that I was crying and laughing at the same time. I can't really explain it. I just felt a deep connection with them.

I blew the kids kisses in the air; me on the street, them on the school buses. The kids stuck out their tongues at me and laughed so hard they fell off of the seats. Then their teacher came over with a big smile and started speaking to me in Hebrew. "You must be from Israel. Are you from Jerusalem?" he asked me. I couldn't believe it.

"How do you know?" I answered him in Hebrew.

He had a big smile on his face and said, "I've seen this before. It's been years since I've seen it, but you must be from Jerusalem if you're acting like this." Then he gave me a big hug and told me he needed to see me blowing kisses in the air to the kids more than I needed to blow the kisses. I kissed him on the cheek and told him I loved him. I was just overwhelmed with a love for the Jewish People; my people.

I kept walking for an hour. I knew it would take an hour to walk back. I went into stores, bought some coffee and pastries, then went into a toy store and bought "Mitzvoh Kinder" (*mitzvah kids*), which were little plastic dolls of kids with *tzitziot* and *kippot*. I bought them for my wife, who studied Yiddish. She had asked me to see if I could find them on my trip. What a surprise to find them so easily. I went into bookstores and just about any store to see the

Jews working and buying there. After an hour I started walking back; taking in all of the buildings and the people.

Sometime on *Shabbos* my friend and I were talking about where he was going to stay after the wedding. He told me it was a secret location and he couldn't tell me. His future wife didn't want anyone to know where they would be staying on their wedding night.

I told him, "No problem. I'm staying at the Hyatt Hotel in Midtown." He couldn't believe it.

"No way. That's where we're staying." Now I couldn't believe it. He told me he promised to get his future wife a room in a beautiful Manhattan hotel and picked this one. We joked how funny it would be if we ran into each other in the hotel lobby after the wedding. Then he realized it wouldn't be so funny since it was meant to be a "secret location."

When I arrived at the hotel, I asked the guy helping me with my bags if he'd seen a bride and groom come in before me. "No, not yet." He asked the other people at the front desk and they also hadn't seen them. He put my bags on the trolley and, just as we were heading up to my room, my friend and his wife showed up with their stretch limousine. The hotel worker looked at me like I could tell the future. I told him I was just at their wedding and I knew they were staying here.

Now, I asked myself, what do I do? Do I say "hi" to my friend and let his wife know that I know the "secret location" or get in the elevator before they have a chance to see me? But just then my friend saw me. He had such a big smile on his face so I ran over and feigned surprise. I gave him a hug, wished his wife a "mazal tov" and told the dismayed guy with the baggage to get us out of there as fast as possible. The whole way to my room he kept saying, "I can't believe it. How did you know?" even though I had told him already.

The next morning I looked on my iPad where the closest shul (synagogue) was. It turned out it was a five-minute walk from the hotel and *davening* was starting in fifteen minutes. I asked the front desk how to get there as I headed out with my *tallis* and *tefillin* bag.

On the way I ran into Rabbi Adin Steinsaltz. Rabbi Steinsaltz is one of the greatest Jewish scholars and rabbis of our generation. His international headquarters is right down the street from where I live in Jerusalem. I see the rabbi occasionally on the street and always say "shalom aleichem" (peace unto you) when I see him. What a surprise it was to run into Rabbi Steinsaltz on the street in Manhattan.

He had his head down. I stood in front of him and said in Hebrew, "Rabbi Steinsaltz. Shalom aleichem. What are you doing here in Manhattan? I'm Barak Hullman. I live in Nachlaot." He's a short man. He looked up at me squinting and said, "Good for you," then kept walking.

After arriving at the shul, I opened my bag to put on my *tallis* and *tefillin*, only to discover my shofar was gone. I thought back to what could have happened. The bag had been closed since the previous morning when we *daven*ed at 770. Then I realized I had left it on the bench at 770. I couldn't believe it; I'd had that shofar for thirty-one years. I blew it every year, and now I lost it and I knew that, even if I had the time to go back to 770, there was no way I would find the shofar. There were countless shofars floating around on the benches and tables at 770. Someone would have thought it was one of the communal shofars and put it in the pile.

My shofar was gone and it hit me hard. It was the only item I still had from my youth. It was an exercise in letting go of something that was never actually mine. I had about six hours in Manhattan until I needed to catch my flight back to Israel.

The first thing on my list was to get a new shofar. I needed it for the next day when I would be *davening* in the airport in London. After shul, I searched online for the "largest Judaica store in Manhattan." I got an address and headed there on foot.

I reached the Judaica store and asked where the shofars were. There were hundreds of them, all with colored dot price stickers. I had just sold a website of mine a few days earlier for $5,000. I decided I would spend up to $500 on a new shofar. Since the most expensive shofar was $350, I had an unlimited shofar budget.

I first tried some random shofars that caught my attention, but then I realized I had to try every single shofar if I wanted to make a purchase and not regret it. There were over two hundred shofars. I asked the woman at the entrance if it was okay to try blowing all of the shofars and she said that she didn't mind. I blew every single one of them. I started categorizing them based on how they sounded until I got down to three. Then I blew the full *seder* (series) of shofar blows over and over until I decided on the one that I wanted. I took it to the cashier; an older looking woman who was clearly Jewish.

The first thing she said to me was, "Where you are from? You're not from around here." I told her I'd lived in Jerusalem for more than twenty years now. "I can tell right away that you're not from around here. Do you want to know how?"

I really didn't know how to answer her. "Of course. I don't even know what you're talking about."

Then she told me, "I've never heard the shofar blown like that."

Then she shouts out to her co-worker in the back of the store and he shouts back, "Tell him not to stop blowing the shofar!" There was a non-Jewish woman standing next to the woman at the cash register. She had this look on her face like she'd just experienced something profound. All I did was blow two hundred or so shofars.

The woman gave me a discount on the shofar and then she told me, "Get on a plane back to Israel today and never come back here again. I don't ever want to see you in my store again. You are too special of a soul to be living in a place like New York." Then she thanked me again for blowing all of the shofars. I left happy that I had gotten a discount and a little confused as to what I did to make everyone in the store feel that way.

Within a few hours I was headed to London to connect to my airplane back to Israel. When I arrived it was early in the morning, just in time to start *davening* again. This time I had my new shofar. It's a little different blowing the shofar in London, Heathrow than it is in New York. But I had to blow the shofar. So, when I finished *davening*, I blew it. I thought, they must see all kinds of strange things at Heathrow. I'm sure they've seen someone blowing the shofar before.

At first I tried to blow it softly, but this shofar has a great sound; an even better sound than my old one and it can't be blown softly. So, I realized, I'm a Jew, I'm proud to be a Jew. I'm getting on that plane in a few minutes. Blow the shofar and change the world. I stood in the corner and blew the shofar as loud as I could. Everyone stopped for a second to see what was going on. Was it an alarm? A fire? It was both. I was both.

LIKE YOUR WISDOM TEETH

The days go by. The Alter Rebbe of Chabad said that one long summer day and one long winter night is an entire year. Many times the Jewish holidays come and I'm totally unprepared. But they come regardless. Some of the holidays require real preparation, such as Pesach and Sukkot. On Pesach, the house has to be kashered and the food prepared; for Sukkot the sukkah has to be built and the *lulav* and *etrog* purchased.

Most of the time the merry-go-round of life is moving so fast I'm not ready at all for a holiday. I'm still waiting to get a break from all the spinning around. *Shabbos* comes every week. Like it or not, ready or not, it comes and that's it. No work, no using electricity, no cooking. Everything has to be ready or you're in big trouble. I've already gotten used to *Shabbos*. Many times I start preparing for the next *Shabbos* the day after *Shabbos* ends.

Shabbos comes every week, but those holidays can creep up on you like a kid hiding behind the bushes waiting to throw a water balloon at you when you walk by. It's not just the holidays that I'm unprepared for, it's the kids too. They grow up whether you're ready for it or not.

We had so many plans on how we were going to raise them and then, when we actually raised them, they partially raised themselves. You do what you can. You give them as much as you can and then they're grown up. With us, we still have plenty of little kids so it's not all lost. It seems like we did a good job with the oldest. She's fourteen going on eighteen. They grow up fast.

How about us adults? We also grow up fast. We're always chasing something: money, health, relationships, the next accomplishment, paying off debts, buying a house… you name it. And along the way, the kids grow up and the holidays come. Before we know it, ten years have passed; maybe longer.

When I was younger, things went by slower. The years between 1st and 6th grade took forever. In 6th grade going on 7th, transitioning from elementary school to Jr. High School, I wondered how I would ever make it to 12th grade. It seemed impossible, but I made it. It's not like I did anything. No, literally. I slept through most of high school. I was awake for other things during high school. Each year I did just well enough not to be held back a grade and before I knew it I had graduated.

Not everyone made it out of my high school. There was one girl who had been with me since elementary school that died in a car crash in my last year. Her name was Michelle Gerber. She was one of those kids everyone made fun of in elementary school. I didn't see what was so bad about her. Then, by the time she got to high school she found friends who liked her. They weren't the greatest crowd—heavy metal rock music and drugs. But she had friends and, because our high school was so big, she could leave that strange reputation behind. Her years moved faster than mine.

Life is like this. It just goes by, whether we're ready for it or not. The good times go by too fast. The bad times pass eventually. There's always a better day tomorrow and, if not, there's the day after that. It's just waiting there like your wisdom teeth. It will come whether you're ready or not.

SO MUCH FOR THE "SOCIAL CONTRACT"

Igraduated from Rutgers College as an honors student and I couldn't find a job. I had studied History and Middle Eastern Languages but had no clue what to do after graduation. I knew I wanted to go to graduate school, but I wasn't ready right after finishing my undergraduate studies. I looked for jobs, however I wasn't qualified for anything except working in an optical store thanks to my family's business. Unfortunately, there were no optical jobs available.

I applied for a job as a waiter at a Mexican restaurant and was rejected because I was "overqualified." The owner told me, "You college kids never stick around. I want someone who is going to work here for years. You kids, once you find a better job, you're out of here." I almost convinced him to give me the job, but the truth is that he was right. I would have left as soon as I found a better job. That's what I did after I got a job at Sizzler's. The only job a kosher vegetarian found was at a national steakhouse chain. It was my first time working in a restaurant.

I learned to appreciate how hard it is to work in and run a restaurant; coming to appreciate the old time waitresses for whom this was really a profession and not just a holdover job until they found something better.

I kept interviewing at the local optical chains trying to get a better paying, less physical job. After a month I landed a job at Pearl Optical repairing glasses.

I grew up working in my father's optical store since I was in kindergarten. It was a short walk from my elementary school. My grandmother worked there as well; a real family business. I worked at my father's store until I was nineteen and left for Rutgers College. My father loved to say that he had three generations of Hullmans working in his store. He even eventually made TV ads with the three generations of Hullmans.

Initially, my father gave me small tasks to do. As the years went by the tasks got more sophisticated. Eventually, at thirteen years old, I was working in his lab, using all of the equipment to make glasses from start to finish. By the time I was sixteen, I was almost a master at the craft. My father was a very good teacher and I learned more about running a small business than any school could have taught me. My father always told me that he was giving me an invaluable education.

A funny thing happened when I worked at these chain businesses. For some reason, the workers there always wanted to know if I was a corporate spy. By then I was wearing a kippah all the time. Did they really think corporate headquarters would hire someone who sticks out like a religious Jew to spy on their employees?

After I convinced my new co-workers that I wasn't a spy, they decided to try to freak out the oldest employee in the store, Leon, by telling him that I was indeed a spy. They kept joking with him, "Be careful, Leon, Barak over there is watching you."

Leon would look at me, worried, and say, "Why should I care? He's the new employee."

"No, no, no, Leon," the other workers would say, "Barak, he's a corporate spy. He can get any of us fired with just a phone call to corporate headquarters." This went on for days. The staff begged me not to tell Leon that I wasn't a spy. I didn't like the game. I wasn't certain, but I was pretty sure that Leon was a fellow Jew and, regardless, he was an old man that still needed to work. Growing up in South Florida, I came to love and respect older people. The last thing I wanted was to stress out Leon.

One day we were in the lunchroom and the staff was making fun of Leon again. They insisted he shouldn't even as much look at me because one wrong stare and I'd get him fired. Finally, Leon confronted me in the lunchroom. "Are you a spy? Tell me. I have to know!" Behind him was the staff smiling, laughing, making faces and hand signals, and begging me not to tell him the truth. I didn't know what to do. Before I could tell him that I wasn't, the staff took over to keep me from revealing the secret. Eventually Leon said to me, "*Emes*? Is it the *emes*?"

Now I knew he was a Jew. Leon knew that I would know the Yiddish word for "truth." Of course, the non-Jewish workers had no idea what he was saying. "It's not the *emes*," I said. The whole time the staff was trying to figure out what was going on.

"What did he say?" they asked me. "What's *emes*?" But I didn't need to answer. They could see the relief on Leon's face. "Oh, man," you could hear them all saying together, "you told him!"

After three months at Pearl, I was looking to make more money. I landed a better paying, more interesting job at Lenscrafters working in their lab. My father had a lab in his office, but it was nothing compared to Lenscrafters. At my father's store, we would order lenses from a lab in Miami, but here they *made* the lenses from scratch from blocks of plastic. I picked up the skill quickly and could then make eyeglasses from start to finish. These days, computers and mini robots have taken over the skills I learned as a kid, but back then it was still a manual job.

Working for these corporations taught me a sad lesson. When you work for a small business, you know everything that's happening and you can feel how important you are for the business to succeed. When I worked for corporations I realized that I was just a number. My paycheck had my number. My employee statistics posted in the lunchroom had my number. I was just a number.

Each lab around the country had a number too and we were ranked nationwide, statewide, and by region. Every new job in the lab had a barcode. You would login to each station of the lab as the eyeglasses made their way through the assembly process. Lenscrafters built their business on the guarantee of "your glasses in an hour or they're free."

In my father's store we would take a day or two to make the glasses. By the time I was in high school and had a car, I would come to my father's lab after the store was closed in the evenings and work for hours in the back, making the glasses. There was no pressure.

But at Lenscrafters there was a lot of pressure. It was better to finish an order and have it be wrong—as long as it was finished within an hour—than to take your time and do it right. As a result, a lot of times we rushed to finish all of the orders, only to discover that the right and left lens were switched or the prescription was off. But we *had to finish the job within an hour*. It was do or die. It made the employees miserable.

We were constantly ranked as the worst lab in the entire country. If we had ranked better we would have all received bonuses. We tried, but we just couldn't seem to work together well enough to pull out of last place. Every week the national results would be posted in the lunchroom and every week we were the worst or the second to worst lab in the country. Not far from us, in Princeton, New Jersey (the city where the university is), there was one of the best labs in the country. Someone at corporate decided to give a promotion to the assistant lab manager at the Princeton store and make him the manager of our lab.

He was a young guy, probably twenty-two, just like I was at the time. He got a big raise, bought himself a beautiful red sports car, and came into our lab as the hotshot who was going to turn things around. He made it clear to us on the first day that we were pathetic and he was awesome. His job was to show us how to be awesome like him.

He stood over our shoulders, shouting at us to work faster, losing his temper, pulling jobs away from us "idiots" so he could finish them himself. It got to the point where he was running the entire lab himself while we watched him to "learn how it's done right." We were all highly skilled employees; we didn't need a boss to yell at us. We needed someone who would build a team.

At first I went with the flow like everyone else in the lab. We'd make fun of the new boss behind his back. We'd still follow the old boss who was demoted to assistant lab manager. He took it well. He kept telling me how he was looking for a better job, maybe working at UPS. When I'd ask him why he'd leave a skilled profession to be a delivery guy, his answer was simple, "It pays more."

After a few weeks of being yelled at every day at work, I lost my patience. I gently told the new boss that his methods weren't working. "Don't tell me how to run a lab," he'd say. "I know how a real lab runs. I worked for the best lab in the country until I came here to be with you bunch of losers." It didn't take long until the lab results for last place got worse each week. We were actually competing with ourselves for last place by posting worse and worse results every week. The new manager was called in to find out what was going on. He told corporate to give him a little more time and he'd whip us into shape. They gave him more time.

Being a religious Jew, I didn't work on Friday nights or Saturdays. They didn't like that at Lenscrafters, but I always worked a double shift on Sundays, which they did like. One Sunday, after working sixteen hours straight, I was cleaning up the lab and knocked over a bucket of solvent used for making lenses.

The new manager freaked out. He started yelling at me, calling me names, cursing me out. He told me to "clean up the mess" and now, because of me, he'd "have to go to another store and get more solvent for the morning." That was my breaking point. I lost it. I was exhausted, having spent weeks being yelled at and abused.

I cursed him out in Hebrew. I went on and on telling my boss what an idiot he was and all along he had no idea what I was saying. But even though he didn't understand the words he understood what I was doing. Afterwards I calmed down and went back to cleaning up the mess.

The rest of the staff was now staring at the two of us. It was like watching the lions in the zoo fighting with each other. We were in the lab behind a wall of glass so everyone could see. The boss told me to get out of there and don't come back tomorrow. I happily left him to clean up the mess.

The next day I stayed home. I was living with my girlfriend at the time. She had a tech support job at a large law firm. She left for work and I started reading a book. A few hours later I got a phone call from the general manager of the Lenscrafters store, who

I hardly ever spoke with. She asked me to come in and go straight to her office when I arrived. I came in and waited; she asked me to tell her what happened.

I told her how the lab manager had no idea how to manage employees; how we all hated him; and how he yelled at us all day. She amazed me when she said, "If that's true, how come no one else on the staff has complained? They all tell me the new manager is doing a great job." I was blindsided. That was the last thing I expected to hear. Then I realized, they all needed their jobs. They needed it to pay their mortgages; to feed their kids. I didn't need this job. It was just a stepping stone to the next thing for me.

Then they brought in my boss and he blamed me for all of the problems in the lab. If they'd just fire me, everything would be great. I argued for the job. I even told them to promote me to be the lab manager. I was laughed out of the office and was told to wait outside for a few minutes. The assistant manager went in. Then after about fifteen minutes the door opened and I was called back in. "Do you have anything else to add?"

"Well, actually, I do," and I started telling them about the book I was reading; *Leviathan*, by Thomas Hobbes. I told them about the "social contract" and explained how the manager really needed to treat us all better or we'd rebel.

At some point the general manager interrupted me and said, "Okay, we've heard enough." Looking me in the eye, she said, "You're terminated." I was appalled. I really thought they would fire the manager.

It is so much fun to see how naïve I was at twenty-two. I was incredulous. "I'm terminated? What? Like Arnold Schwarzenegger? 'You're terminated?'" I said, imitating the Terminator. They asked me to leave. I could come back in a week to get my final paycheck.

As I was leaving, all the workers wanted to know what had happened. They were surprised when I told them I was "terminated." They all wanted to know why. Was it because of what I said to the lab manager when I was yelling back at him? I just left.

When I came home and told her what happened, my girlfriend was furious at me. I started looking for a new job in the newspapers. I wasn't sure what I was going to do and was fuming. I was so upset at the injustice. *I* was fired? *He* should have been fired, not me.

The week passed and I had already applied for several programs in Israel. I was going to Israel to live my dream, after going back to Lenscrafters to pick up the final paycheck. As I drove in I could see all of the employees looking at me through the large bay windows. I parked in the middle of the parking lot; employees were not supposed to take up the front spaces. Everyone was watching me as I came into the store. I could see they still hadn't found someone to replace me in the lab and the lab manager was yelling at everyone just like before.

Now I was free. I didn't have to take his abuse. I was immune. Everyone asked how I was doing. I went and picked up my check, shaking from anger as I got back in my car. I could see the lab manager in the large bay windows facing the parking lot. There he was, running the lab and here I was unemployed sitting in my rundown car. I looked at his fancy, red, new sports car, then began to watch him in the lab. I couldn't take the injustice of it all.

I had this crazy idea. I wanted to run into the side of his car. He made sure to park it somewhere where no one else would park so it wouldn't get a scratch. That made it an easy target for me. There were no cars blocking my path. As I slowly drove out of the parking lot, I looked at his shiny, new, red sports car and then sped up and crashed right into the passenger door. I could hardly believe I was going to do this and, before I knew it, I had hit the lab manager's car. My car just kind of lunged forward; like a lion pouncing on his prey. I felt good. It was a pleasure.

But a second later, I didn't feel so good. "Oh my God!" I yelled to myself in the car, and then I drove out of the parking lot as fast as possible. On my way out I could see the entire store had been watching me from the large windows. A lot of them had huge smiles on their faces. Some were even patting each other on their backs and pointing at me.

I went home and locked the door, not knowing what to do now. I couldn't believe what I had done. My anger had reached a really low point. So much for the "social contract." I had just crumbled it up and thrown it in the fire.

About an hour later there was a knock at the door. I ignored it. I didn't want to talk with anyone now. Then there was the knock again and again. It was loud and strong. I decided to see who was there. When I checked in the peephole I saw a uniformed policeman. He banged again while I was looking in the peephole; I decided to answer the door. "Are you Barak Hullman?" he asked, angrily. I really had no idea what was going on. "Did you work at Lenscrafters?" he asked. Then I knew what was going on.

He told me that everyone had witnessed me hitting my boss's car and that I was under arrest for a hit and run. He took out his handcuffs. "Whoa. Wait a minute." I told him, "You're arresting me?"

"Yes, sir," he told me, authoritatively.

"What? For bumping into my boss's car while I left the parking lot?" I asked.

"You didn't bump into your boss's car. It was an intentional hit and run. Turn around, sir. You're under arrest."

I told him I just got fired and my boss called the cops on me. He just hates me. I didn't hit his car—but the officer seemed a little confused. "Okay, I'm not going to arrest you, but I'm setting a court date for you. You'll explain it to the judge." He wrote up a ticket and left. I called my girlfriend at the law office. How do I get out of this one?

She was furious at me. It was a theme with her. She asked around and when she came home that night told me what to do, saying that the lawyers said to take pictures of my boss's car and then take them to an auto shop. Get an estimate on how much it would cost to fix it. They said to take pictures from lots of angles until you found ones that didn't make it look so bad.

A few days later I found the nerve to go back to the parking lot. You can imagine the shock on my ex-coworkers' faces when they saw me. My ex-boss came running out into the parking lot screaming at me. I ignored him as I slowly took around a hundred pictures of his car from every angle I could. He called the police. The store manager came out and told me I had to leave. I was gone in about ten minutes.

I quickly took the film for one-hour developing and then started getting quotes to fix the damage. To my shock and surprise, the ex-boss's car was really well built to withstand a side hit. There was hardly a scratch on his car, though my front bumper didn't look so great. I received low quotes to fix the dent and the paint: around $100. One auto shop told me they'd do it for free. I had them put it in writing and went home feeling confident.

The court date came a few weeks later. I wore a suit, bought specifically for the court date. I also wore my *tzitziot* (religious strings) out for the first time. I noticed the judge had a Jewish name, Harry Cohen, and I was hoping he would have compassion on a fellow Jew. I know it usually works the other way. I showed up in the morning for my appointed time and waited for my turn. Hours passed and they still hadn't called me.

I asked a clerk if I was on the docket and he said yes. I asked what was going on and he said, "Just wait until your name is called, sir." I was there from 9 am until 3 pm. My case was called for 10 am. Finally, at the end of the court day, the prosecutor came over to me and said that they were still waiting for the plaintiff to appear.

The officer who came to arrest me had been waiting for hours. He looked angry. I could tell he was going to make sure I got in trouble for what I did. The prosecutor and the defender both asked to see my evidence. I showed them the pictures and the quotes, telling them it was a mistake. They looked at each other and said, "Okay, we got it."

The judge called for my ex-boss to present himself. He called again and again. My ex-boss wasn't there. He asked that we all wait for him to appear. Finally, when the court was meant to end, he told me, "It's your lucky day, son. Since the plaintiff didn't show up we can't prosecute you. Go home and don't do something stupid like that again."

I was relieved, of course. However, I wasn't very happy about what I had done. All of the emotional stress that came along with the firing and the court case had exhausted me. I wasn't angry at my old boss any more. My future was never at Lenscrafters, but somewhere else on the horizon. I still hadn't found it or created it. But for my ex-boss, maybe that was it, the last stop on the line. I also realized that I needed to learn to control my anger.

I'm still working on it more than twenty years later. I've gotten a lot better and this incident became a red line for me not to cross again. A lot of times I go through life like a first-person shooter game, not realizing that other people are watching and affected by me. When I get angry, I just think of how I crossed the line when I hit my boss's car. It keeps me calm. Most of the time.

SO WHY ARE YOU DRIVING ON SHABBOS?

I didn't grow up in a very religious home. We were connected to our synagogue and the Jewish religion, but still lived a very secular life. Our life was religious in the shul, secular outside. We kept some holidays. Others we kind of acknowledged but didn't keep. Over time I grew more and more religious, but it was a gradual process.

For a long time I did a little of this and little of that. For example, when I came back from my first visit to Israel, the one external thing I decided to bring back was wearing a kippah. It identified me as a religious Jew even though I wasn't. I was a Jew; a proud Jew, but I didn't keep kosher. I didn't keep *Shabbos*. I didn't *daven*. I didn't put on *tefillin*. I didn't learn Torah. I pretty much didn't do anything except wear a kippah all the time. So people assumed I was religious.

I would walk into a "kosher style" restaurant and the owner would scream, "It's not kosher here!" I'd tell him I know and I don't keep kosher.

"Well, then why are you wearing a kippah?"

"I just like to," I would say. But it really bothered people.

I grew up in South Florida with a lot of old Jews. They didn't keep kosher, but many of them grew up keeping kosher. For them, seeing a young man in a kippah meant he kept kosher, and here I was in a non-kosher restaurant that sold kosher-style food. They sold the food that Eastern European Jews ate, but without following the laws of kashrut.

One time I walked into a bagel shop that wasn't kosher with my kippah on. Most of the clientele were old Jews. As I walked to my seat, one after another called me over to their table. As I went over, the whole table would say, "You can't wear that thing in here," referring to my kippah, "it's not kosher."

"I know it's not kosher," I'd say. "I don't really care." They didn't get it.

"So, why are you wearing a kippah?" they'd ask me.

"Because I like to," was always my answer.

"But it's not kosher here."

"So why are *you* eating here?" I'd respond.

Over and over again, table after table of old, sweet Jews. "Boychik, come over here." I'd go over to the table. Sometimes they'd say it out loud; sometimes they'd say it in a whisper, "It's not kosher here."

"I know," I'd whisper back. And then we'd go through the whole script again, "So why are *you* eating here?"

I wonder if anyone questioned themselves afterwards. If they cared so much about me and my kippah, maybe they really shouldn't have been eating there?

I had several Jewish teachers in my public high school. They saw me come back from the semester in Israel wearing a kippah. When they saw me eating the non-kosher food in the school cafeteria, they told me, "You know, it's not kosher there." I knew, of course I knew, and I didn't really care. "But you're wearing a kippah."

After a few weeks, one teacher who kept kosher begged me not to wear my kippah in school. I don't know why I listened to her, but I started wearing my kippah from the time I woke up in the morning until I reached the school parking lot. Then I'd take it off in my car, walk into school and, when the day ended, the first thing I would do when I stepped into my car was put my kippah back on.

Often I would drive on *Shabbos*. Why not? I didn't keep the laws of the Jewish Sabbath. And I would wear my kippah. At times people would honk their horns at me at a traffic light and motion to roll down the window. I obliged. "What?" I'd ask.

"It's *Shabbos*," they'd say.

"I know it's *Shabbos*. Of course, I know."

"Then why are you driving on *Shabbos*?" when driving on *Shabbos* was forbidden.

I'd always give the same answer, "Why are *you* driving on *Shabbos*?"

When I got to Rutgers College and started attending the Chabad House, I would go to the services on Friday night and then afterwards go to the local pizzeria and get some non-kosher pizza. I had a female friend who liked this and would join me Friday nights in shul and then come with me to the pizzeria afterwards. This was my Friday night for several months. Then I decided to stay at the Chabad House for dinner. Come *Shabbos*/Saturday morning, I would treat it like a regular day. But eventually I started going to services on Saturday morning as well. Then I got to the point where I'd stay the whole day, having both the Friday night and afternoon meals at the Chabad House. Eventually, my friend joined me.

But I still drove on *Shabbos* and I still ate in non-kosher restaurants. All the time I would spend most of my *Shabbos*es at the Chabad House. I left for a year to study in Edinburgh. When I came back I was ready to do more, Jewishly. I still drove on *Shabbos* with my kippah. But one *Shabbos*, I drove into Manhattan for a reason I don't remember. I felt like I was driving myself away from the peace of mind I had when I stayed by the Chabad House. I had obligated myself to be where I was going that Saturday, but the whole ride I felt like something was wrong. It was like a switch had been flipped inside of me.

When I'm keeping *Shabbos*, I feel bliss. It's like I'm high on *Shabbos*. When I drove on *Shabbos*, it was just like a regular weekday. I want the bliss. I want to be high on *Shabbos*. I decided I would no longer drive on *Shabbos* again.

These days I wait the whole week for *Shabbos* to come. All that time when I was asking people, "So why are *you* driving on *Shabbos*?" or "Why aren't *you* keeping kosher?" I now realize that I was actually asking those questions to myself.

DRUNK ON PURIM

Some people think this world is hell. This world is actually full of beauty and beautiful moments. It's there for you to tap into for as long as you allow yourself.

We all have problems. We all have situations that are totally out of our control. Sometimes we allow these moments to dominate our lives.

When I'm conscious enough, I can tap into the beauty of the moment. Sometimes it's looking at the sky or stars. I love to look at the clouds and see what God's painting today. I especially like looking at the stars on a winter night. In the mornings, part of my weekday routine is going to the juice stand in the Shuk (open air market) and watching people as I drink my juice. I see all kinds of people. I don't know anything about them. Most of them, I'll never see in my life again. They're just there, in my life, for that moment.

Most people don't notice me looking at them from the juice stand. Sometimes they do and they'll look back. I wonder what they're thinking about me.

I catch people in their happy moments; a group of friends together laughing or excited. Sometimes I'll see a person carrying flowers or balloons. It's pretty clear when it's their birthday and they're the one that received the flowers or if they're bringing the flowers to someone else. Almost every single person I've observed has a clear purpose and direction in life. At least at *that moment* they know exactly where they're going or where they want to be.

Years ago I got drunk on Purim and started hugging everyone.

I even hugged the Arab-Muslim gardener in our neighborhood. I actually remember kissing him and telling him in Arabic how much I love him. I hugged people all day and, when the day was over and the alcohol wore off, I was changed forever. I gave off and received so much good energy and love that day, it actually changed me as a person for the better. Now I still hug people. Even though I only get drunk once a year (on Purim), I hug people all year round.

I realized at some point that I can heal people with my hugs. I read a story years ago about a Rebbe who healed a child this way. The parents were at their wit's end. Their son could not concentrate on his studies. He was constantly causing trouble and it got to the point where the parents were worried for his mental health. He was a young child so there wasn't any real reasoning with him. They brought their son to the Rebbe and he took the boy with him into his study and closed the door.

About five minutes later he came out with the boy. He was calm and relaxed. They asked the Rebbe, "What did you do? What did you say?" He told the parents that he knew he couldn't reason with the child so he simply put the child's ear on his chest and hugged him. He said that his *neshama* (soul) spoke to the boy's *neshama* and healed him.

That story blew me away. I thought, what if I could also heal people with my hugs? So, I started trying and, with one person after another, I realized my *neshama* could speak to theirs. I still hug people, but now, almost every person I hug is getting a healing hug. It's a hug that comes from breathing in moments of beauty. I try to live off of these moments. They are my sustenance.

GARBAGE BAGS FILLED WITH MELTED FRAMES

I started working for my father in 2nd grade. His optical store was a short walk from my elementary school. After school I would walk to his office. There really wasn't anything for me to do there. Regardless, my father put me to work. Sometimes I would fill up the candy jars or throw out the garbage. Most of the time I would play with coloring books and read *Highlights* magazine.

I used to walk to school in the mornings with my father. I only found out many years later that the reason my father started walking me to school and himself to work was because his business had burned down. The insurance company would not pay for the damage, so he was penniless. He had to sell his car in order to start up again. I had no idea. One day my parents told me my father would start walking me to school. I just assumed that it was a parent-child bonding.

We lived on Bay Harbor Island in South Florida. It was the island the Jews could live on. The next door island, Bal Harbour, had signs on the stores and hotels saying, "No Dogs. No Niggers. No Jews." Seeing the signs as my father and I were walking into a fancy hotel, I told him we couldn't go in. He said no one paid attention to those signs anymore.

Bal Harbour was connected to Bay Harbor by bridges. We would walk from our island, where we lived, to the island next door where my elementary school was. Along the way we stopped on one of the bridges to look at the baby swordfish below in the crystal clear blue water. We always met this kind, heavy-set policeman on our walk. Everyone knew my father, and we would always talk with the policeman. He insisted he had a watermelon in his stomach, which he asked me to punch. It became part of our daily routine. Look at the fish, punch the policeman in the stomach, and then continue on to school. After school I would walk to my father's office by myself.

By the time I was sixteen I was given more responsibilities. I deposited the cash from that day in the bank account. I stayed late making eyeglasses and drove myself home after everyone had left work. I went with the landlord on the roof to look for leaks and climbed up the ladder to change the air conditioner filters. One of the jobs my father gave me was dealing with a friend of his, Asher. Asher sold dirt cheap eyeglass frames. He'd buy them in bulk from God knows where and sell them to my father and other small businesses like his.

My father never seemed to like Asher, but I did. Asher was eccentric. He was full of energy, wore bright colors, and laughed a lot. My father was serious and didn't have the patience for Asher.

I'd go with Asher behind the store where his car was parked in the scorching South Florida heat and humidity. He'd open the trunk and there would be garbage bags filled with frames. A lot of them were bent and tangled together having melted and warped from the heat. I would sort through them; picking out what I thought would sell. After I took out a few hundred frames, my father would pay Asher and then Asher would hang around talking with me.

Many times my father would shoo Asher away, telling him to leave me alone and let me work. Our relationship developed over the years and I came to like Asher more and more. The feeling was mutual. Asher never had any kids. He always had attractive girlfriends, but never got married. He was still a kid himself. He never grew up.

One time Asher asked to take me out to lunch. I was eighteen at the time. We went to a diner somewhere on South Beach. It was still the old South Beach; nothing like what it is today.

Asher was so excited he could hardly stay in his seat in the booth where we were sitting. He asked me questions like, "Do you have a girlfriend or is there someone you're interested in?" I told him about the girls I liked or dated or wanted to date. "What are your dreams?" he asked. "What do you want to do with your life?"

I asked him "What do you want to do?"

"I have no idea," he said and then continued, "I don't care. I want to hear about you!" I told him about my dreams and he jumped up and down, excited by the answers.

He called over a waitress and told her, "Listen to this kid. Do you hear what he's saying?" The waitress wasn't impressed. He looked at her seriously and said slowly, "Do you remember what it was like to be a kid and have dreams?" She sighed and then listened a bit.

Asher was probably forty-five at the time. Now Asher has passed away and I'm forty-five. I can still picture myself talking with him at that diner and not understanding why he was so excited.

But when I look back at the scene in my mind, I get it. Asher was a genius and a very special friend. Not only did he give himself a glimpse of what it was to be kid and have dreams, he left me with the gift of that memory too.

I CAN SPOT A THIEF
IN ANY LANGUAGE

For a year I was making part of my living by traveling from Jerusalem to the East Coast of the States to sell Judaica and Jewish art made in Israel. I would buy thousands of dollars of artwork and take it with me in two or three suitcases to the US. Once there I would travel from Israel fairs to Jewish events selling the merchandise for a week or two, and then come back to Israel.

On one of my trips I landed at JFK airport in New York. It was winter. After I gathered my suitcases and convinced customs not to tax me on the merchandise, I got in line to wait for a taxi to take me to Manhattan.

I'm a religious Jew and I look like one. After standing in a huge line in the winter cold for about ten minutes, a middle aged man came over to me. He started speaking in Hebrew. He said he had a private town car and asked how much I wanted to pay to go to Manhattan. I told him I preferred to take a taxi.

He insisted. He even took one of my suitcases and started walking toward his car shouting for me to follow him. I asked the person behind me in line to watch my other suitcases while I ran to get my livelihood back from this guy, then I was quickly back in line.

The Israeli town car driver came back and continued begging me to let him drive me to Manhattan. In the meantime, the line was moving forward quickly enough that I didn't mind waiting. There was no way I was going to let this guy take me anywhere. After it was clear to him that I had only ten more minutes or so until the next taxi, he cursed me out and left.

About thirty seconds later, two undercover policemen approached me. Undercover is pretty convincing. I would never, ever have guessed that these guys were undercover cops. They showed me their badges and asked if that guy was harassing me about driving me somewhere for a fare.

Before I had a chance to answer, the Israeli saw what was happening and ran over to us screaming in Hebrew, "Don't tell them anything. Please. Don't say anything!" In the meantime the police told me to ignore him and to tell them "Yes or no? Did he offer to give you a ride for a fare?" The answer was "yes", but the Israeli was going nuts saying to tell them "no." I didn't put two and two together until I said the word "yes" in English to the cops. They quickly turned around and arrested the Israeli.

I asked what was going on. The cops told me it was illegal to take passengers without a license and that their job was to stop this illegal activity at JFK. They thanked me and started taking the Israeli to a police car. As soon as the Israeli heard me say the word "yes" he screamed at me, cursing me, saying that now he had to pay a $250 fine and spend the night in jail. I asked the cops if it was true and, without answering, they thanked me again as they took the Israeli away.

He shouted at me as he was being put in the cop car, saying that this was all my fault and asking what kind of Jewish brother am I. I told him it was his own fault and to blame himself. Then he was gone and it's twelve years later and I'm still thinking about it.

◆

Years before I moved to Israel, I was studying and living in New Jersey. I had a Russian Jewish girlfriend at the time that I thought I would marry. We went into Manhattan on a Sunday. After we got off the train this Israeli approached me speaking Hebrew. I was wearing a kippah which identified me as a religious Jew. I was flattered that someone wanted to speak Hebrew with me.

He told me he was stuck in Manhattan without any money and the Israeli consulate was closed on Sunday. His family was supposed to wire him some cash to Bank Leumi (the Israeli national bank) in Manhattan the next day, but for now he didn't have any money for food or a place to stay. He looked like he was lying, but I couldn't tell.

He insisted that he wasn't lying. He showed me his passport and said I could write down his name. He gave me a phone number and his email address. Then he asked for $50, saying that he would wire the money back to me tomorrow or the next day. He begged and he pleaded. I told him I didn't have any cash on me. He said, "No problem, there's an ATM over there." In the meantime my girlfriend told me she was going off on her own and to meet her at the Metropolitan Museum. I walked with the Israeli to the ATM.

When we got there he had a look on his face like he couldn't believe this was actually happening. I had serious doubts about what I was doing. Then, as I typed in my code to the ATM, he said, "I really need $200. Can you loan me $200?"

I didn't know what to do. I was a poor student; I didn't have that kind of money. On the other hand, maybe he really was desperate? I agreed to give him $125 even though I really couldn't afford to.

He thanked me over and over and promised to pay me back. He gave me his mother's name and phone number in Israel and double checked that the information he gave me about his name, number and email were accurate. He took down my name, number and email and swore he would be in touch. I started walking toward the museum to meet my girlfriend at the appointed time.

"Did you actually give that guy money?" she asked me. When I told her yes, she told me I was insane.

"Why?" I said. "Maybe he really needed the money?"

She started laughing at me. "I came from Russia. I can spot a thief in any language in a second. That guy just stole your fifty dollars."

I was hoping she was wrong, but I had a feeling she was right. Then I told her, "I gave him a hundred and twenty-five, not fifty."

"What?" she said, freaking out. "Are you out of your mind? You should have given the money to me. Buy me something for a hundred and twenty-five dollars instead of giving it to a thief! Well," she said, calming down a little, "I hope you learned your lesson." Deep down I hoped that she was wrong.

A year or so passed. My girlfriend and I had broken up. I spent that year in Israel and now was back in New Jersey studying in graduate school at Princeton. I took the train into Manhattan on a Sunday. As I was leaving the train station the same Israeli approached me. I could not believe my eyes. It was the guy I lent the hundred and twenty-five dollars to. Of course, he never contacted me. All of the information he gave me was fake. Even his mother's number in Israel was not real. I know as I tried to call her. Whereas when I first met this guy he looked respectable, now he was a wreck. His teeth were rotting in his mouth, he hadn't bathed in weeks, and his clothes were ripped and dirty. I assumed he was homeless on the streets.

The Israeli thief started speaking to me in Hebrew just like the first time but he was much more desperate now. My Hebrew was a lot better this time around, having spent the year in Israel in order to become fluent. I let him tell me his sad tale and just stared at him without saying a word. He asked me again if I spoke Hebrew and I told him in Hebrew, "You taught me an important lesson, my friend. I was probably one of your first victims in Manhattan. Do you want to pay back my hundred and twenty-five dollars or should I drag you to the police stand right now?" He was stunned. He turned around and started running so fast there was no way I would have caught him.

◆

A few months ago, it was supposed to snow in Jerusalem. It only snows here once every few years. Snow did fall, but it didn't stick. I was disappointed along with most of Jerusalem's residents. However, there's a little patch of land in a courtyard that I pass through when I walk to shul in the mornings. Whenever it snowed in the past, the snow on this little patch of land would melt slower than the surrounding snow because so little sun reaches it in the courtyard.

The day after the snow, I passed through this little patch of land in the courtyard and saw frost on the weeds growing there. It was so exciting. The next day it warmed up and there was no chance of snow. It didn't even rain. For some strange reason, there was still frost on the weeds in the courtyard. I couldn't understand it until the next day, when I got closer to the "frost," only to discover it was toilet paper from a sewage drain that had overflowed during the storm. There was washed up toilet paper everywhere. That was my "frost." It's still there, months later.

When I look at it, I can think of how naïve I am or how lucky I am. Rebbe Nachman said that it's better to believe everything than to believe nothing. Every morning when I pass by my permanent "frost" I laugh. Just for that it's worth it.

A HUMAN BECOMING

O y vey, do I have problems. I have so many problems it feels like once I solve one of them I discover five more. My poor wife, when she married me, I was hardly the person I wanted to be. I still regret how I behaved in the early years of our marriage. I regret so many things. I've made so many mistakes. But what are you going to do? You can't go back. The past is the past. All I have is the present.

One of my teachers, Rabbi David Aaron, said we're not human beings, but human becomings. There's the person I was last year, five years ago, twenty years ago, and there's the person I am today. The person I am today is a product of the decisions that I made in the past. When the mistakes were bad enough, I took them as a lesson on how I could be better. Most of the time I do actually change.

Once, I was apologizing to my wife for the hundredth time for treating her poorly in the early years of our marriage, when I heard myself say: "The person I am today is the fixing for the person I was in the past." I wasn't who I wanted to be in the past, but now I'm better and I'm working on being who I really want to be. Don't judge me on how I used to be. Judge me on how I am now. And if I'm not who I want to be now, I can be that person already by tomorrow. You don't have to wait long to change who you are. None of us knows how long we'll live, or what quality of life we'll have for how long. All we have is the present. Strive to be the person you always wanted to be. Let the person you are today be the fixing for the person you never really wanted to be in the past.

HOW BEAUTIFUL
MELODIES ARE MADE

Has it ever happened that when things weren't going well and you didn't want to talk with anyone a friend comes over and asks, "How are you doing?"

You answer, "Yeah, OK, not so great. Things could be better." It used to happen to me a lot until I learned a lesson from Rebbe Nachman of Breslov.

Rebbe Nachman said, every time a person asks you, "How are you doing?" it's an opportunity to grow and change. If you say, "Eh, not so great," then at that point you are being judged in heaven and it will continue not to be so great. But if you fake it and say, "Amazing! Life has never been better," then the judgment in heaven will be whatever you say, and things can and will get better.

Rebbe Nachman teaches that when you say, "Things are not so great," God says to Himself, "Oh really? You don't like what you have? Let's make things worse and give you a good reason to complain." The opposite also happens. If you say things are great, even when they're not at all, God says, "He thinks *this* is great? I'll show him what great really is."

You can take this however you like, literally or metaphorically. When I first heard this lesson it really upset me. What kind of way is this for God to act? But then I learned a lesson from Rabbi David Aaron that everything God does is an act of love, even if we can't understand it. All through our *davening* it says that Hashem does something or another out of "love." It says "He chose His nation with love." Ask a Jew in the Holocaust if being part of the chosen nation felt like love and I doubt you would find anyone who would agree. I'm not saying I understand it all of the time, but I just took this lesson at face value.

I decided to give it a try. I've had frustrating times, where I felt trapped with no way out. And then, in the midst of my feeling bad for myself, someone will ask me, "How are you doing?" I want to shout, "Miserable, thank you. And if you don't mind, don't ever ask me again. Miserable is where I am and plan to stay. Now get out of my face before I really get angry at you." But instead, as hard as it is, I'll say, "*Baruch Hashem* [thank God]. Does it get any better than this? This is as good as it gets."

In the beginning I couldn't say it sincerely, but over time I got better and better until I could say it and mean it. Yes, I'm unhappy in general, stuck in a job that I hate, exhausted from raising a large family that I love, live in a messy house (thanks to that same family), threatened by terrorists who want to murder me, and I hate this summer heat but, "Everything is great. Thank God. Does it get any better than this?" It takes practice.

Something miraculous happened. First, saying those words made me feel better, if I repeated them enough times that I actually started to believe them. I have all of these problems, but there are so many other people with worse problems than me. There are people who would switch places with me in a second. What am I complaining about? OK, I'm suffering, but the truth is things are better than I realize. Just step back for a second and look at all of the blessings you have.

You might be broke, but you are making some money. You don't like your weight? Pay more attention to what you eat. There's nothing you can do about the job you hate, but at least you have a job. The kids exhaust you? How many people do you know who can't or don't have kids? And don't the kids make you laugh when nobody and nothing else could? I go on and on until I realize that my life actually is good. That was the first thing that started happening to me.

The second is that other people felt better when I said things were great. They were happy for me. "Man, that's great," they would say, "I'm so happy someone has a good life. My life sucks." Ironically, I then would find myself consoling them. Do you get this? I'm the one in a bad mood, but by saying things are great, the other person starts to share their problems with me. Then I share my secret with them. Things aren't so great, but this lesson… most people are inspired by it.

For me it's been a good investment, and things actually did get better. Repeat something long enough and people start to believe it. It works for yourself too.

The Baal Shem Tov would go around asking Jews how they were doing to give them the opportunity to improve their lives, just like I told you above. One day the Baal Shem Tov walked into a house of Jewish learning (beit midrash) and after asking everyone how they were doing, saw an old Jew sitting in the back learning Torah.

He went over to him and said, "Holy brother, shalom aleichem, how are you doing?" The old Jew ignored him. So, the Baal Shem said it louder, "Holy brother, how are you doing?"

The old man looked up at him and said, "I'm learning, leave me alone," and went back to his learning.

The Baal Shem said to him, "How can you hold back from Hashem his parnasa [livelihood]?"

"What?" the old Jew said, looking up at the Baal Shem. "What are you talking about?"

The Baal Shem answered him, "When someone asks you how are you doing and you answer, 'Thank God,' you give Hashem His livelihood. But by not answering you hold back Hashem's livelihood."

Rebbe Nachman taught us to judge everything and everyone positively. By judging people or even objects positively you can literally raise up a person or improve a situation. He said to focus on the good points. Your foot is hurting you? Judge it positively. Say, "Foot, I love you. You've carried me my whole life. I don't know what I would do without you. Have a refuah shelaimah [full recovery] my sweet foot." The same with people.

My son had two teachers in school in 5th grade. One teacher loved him and judged him positively. The other was bitter and regretted any love he shared with my son (I know because he told me himself, many times). When I went for a parent-teacher meeting, the first teacher who judged my son positively, said only good things and how good my son was. My son had no discipline issues in his class and loved this teacher. The second teacher had constant problems with my son. My son didn't understand why the teacher treated him differently than the teacher who loved him.

The first teacher actually spoke with the second one and shared this idea with him. The second teacher tried for a couple of days to find the good in my son, but as soon as my son bothered him, he lost it and told me he regretted any compliments he gave him. Every time my son's second teacher judged him harshly, he ended ⌐ting me for help. I told him, "Judge my son positively and ⌐nges for the better," but some people have a hard ⌐n.

Rebbe Nachman said, "How are beautiful melodies made? By picking out the good notes from the bad." It's just like finding the good traits over the bad.

When I first moved to Israel, I struggled with the language and culture. It took me many years until I realized I was judging everyone and everything harshly. The people didn't have manners; the streets were dirty; the police never helped. The list went on and on. I even had "complaining sessions" where I would sit with other immigrant friends and we would curse and complain.

Once I was in line at the airport with my mother and wife. We were at the early check-in, checking in my mother's bags. I was complaining about how things in Israel are terrible. Eventually someone ahead of us in line turned around and yelled at me, "I'm glad you're leaving this country. We don't need people like you here." Of course, he didn't know that I live here and that I wasn't going anywhere, but that outburst really had an impact on me. It's like the moment when someone says you're an alcoholic or addicted to gambling and you realize that they're right.

It took me a few years until I learned Rebbe Nachman's lesson, to judge even the Land of Israel positively. Boy, I thought to myself, how do I do that? And then I realized, just like everything else.

The garbage in the streets? It's Jewish garbage with Hebrew writing. There's never been anything like that in the history of the world. Look at this miracle. The Jewish people have been restored to their ancient homeland and are speaking a language that had virtually disappeared off the face of the earth. This garbage is a modern day miracle and I'm looking at it right now.

The impolite people? We must love each other so much. Only

family feels so comfortable to be able to treat each other like this.

I found ways to judge everything positively. It's not that I became a doormat and let people walk all over me. I stood my ground; I had opinions and shared them. But I taught myself how to judge everyone and everything positively.

I once had a big problem with an old neighbor many years ago. We moved into our house with one cute kid and a baby. Now we have seven cute kids. The house never grew, but the kids did. We still have just one bathroom. My kids have learned how to share that bathroom; sometimes though, they ended up peeing on the floor.

My neighbor hated us. He hated the noise, the mess, the smell... you name it. We made him crazy. He blamed us for all of his problems. Why couldn't he sell his house? It was because of us. Why did the paint peel on his walls outside of his house, it was my kids' fault.

I never hated or even disliked him. For a long time I would say "hello" to him and he just ignored me. This went on for a long time. I tried to be nice to him, and he would ignore me. Then, if he would ever speak with me, it would be a long list of complaints.

He actually never spoke with me; he yelled at me, at times with spit coming out of his mouth and his face turning red. I knew he had a hard life. He was divorced or a widower with three kids that caused him a lot of grief. He didn't have much money. He was bitter and angry at other people too, but not like he was with us.

I tried to judge him positively for years. I tried to do nice things for him like throwing out his garbage. "Don't *touch* my garbage!" he'd shout at me.

"I'm just trying to do something nice for you. I don't mind. I'm going to the garbage anyway." He hated me.

I asked my rabbi what to do. I told him how for years I've been trying to judge my neighbor positively and he hates me more every year that passes. "That's all you can do," he told me. "Just keep judging him positively." I kept this up for about ten years. Ten years of being ignored, yelled at, cursed, and hated with a passion by my neighbor. Then one day I said "Good morning" to him, and he said, "Good morning" back. I could not believe it. I called my wife and told her. It was like digging for oil for ten years and we had just discovered a little black mud in our deep pit.

We had good days and bad days. It was a transition. Sometimes he'd ignore me. Sometimes he'd yell at me. Sometimes the "Good morning" was bitter, cold and heartless. But eventually he started having a conversation with me. Then he told me my kids were well behaved. I could not believe my ears. It's been a couple of years now that he's treated me nicely. He hasn't yelled at me since. I think he actually likes me. If he ever asks me how I'm doing, I know exactly how to answer him. "Thank God. It's never been so good. Does it get better than this?"

BRONSKY FAST LIFE

It's pretty rare that we visit my in-laws in Haifa for the simple reason that it's hard and expensive to move a family of seven kids anywhere. We have to rent a nine seater van and drive for hours on unsafe, narrow roads. It's also not the highest spiritual experience.

I've been visiting my in-laws' shul for over twenty years now. The last visit was the first time I ever felt so comfortable in their shul. I've grown older and so has everyone else there. But, not everyone lives so long.

In the pew behind my father-in-law's seat in shul was a family whose name is still on the plaques above their seats; Bronsky. It's written in Hebrew without vowels so I'm not sure if it's Bronsky, Bransky or some other variation. Bronsky had a big family, at least eight kids, probably more like ten or eleven, maybe even more. They're all grown and married now. Bronsky's kids moved to other parts of the country. They became too religious for that shul. Even though they don't *daven* there anymore, the plaques on the pews remain. A reminder that they were once there.

I remember the father and kids twenty years ago. There were a lot of kids, and the father was such a character. He had a strange trait that I've rarely seen in anyone else since: he did everything fast. When I say fast, I mean really fast. He spoke fast; he ate fast; he walked fast; he wiped his kids' noses fast; he got angry fast and calmed down fast and, of course, he *daven*ed fast.

My in-laws' entire community was at our wedding. Two packed buses brought them all down to Jerusalem. At the time, I didn't know these people. There were around three hundred people at my wedding, and I could count the ones I knew on my ten fingers. Now, in retrospect, knowing that community, I realize how special it was for them all to come to our wedding.

It had been a long day, our wedding day. In Jewish tradition, many people fast the day of their wedding. The weddings are after sunset and on our wedding day there was a huge winter rainstorm. It was pouring cats and dogs. We were married in a yeshiva parking lot that was covered with a large plastic tent. There was an air heating system pumping hot air into the tent, but the electricity kept going out. You would hear the plastic tubing blowing up like a New Year's Eve party favor as the hot air came back in after the electricity returned.

At the end of the wedding party someone needed to lead *birkat hamazon*, the blessing said after eating bread. The buses to Haifa were leaving. Everyone was exhausted. We needed someone to lead the *bentching* (the blessing) and Bronsky was asked if he would lead it. Realizing that his natural talent to do things fast was finally going to be appreciated, he started the blessing fast and finished it even faster. I don't think I'd ever seen anyone *daven* that fast in my life, not before and not since. We all appreciated it since it's a long prayer and we all wanted to go home.

My in-laws told my wife that the community was so inspired by the joy at our wedding that they sang the whole two-hour ride back to Haifa.

A few years after our wedding, Bronsky passed away quite young. I'm not sure exactly the age, but he was in his early fifties. It was a shock to everyone, including me. It had been at least six months after he had died before we visited my in-laws again. When

I asked my father-in-law where was Bronsky, I was shocked to hear he had passed away.

On this last visit I had a realization. Bronsky was gone. His kids had moved on. But Bronsky's redeeming quality was that he did everything fast. He spoke fast; he ate fast; he walked fast; he wiped his kids' noses fast; he got angry fast and calmed down fast and, of course, he *daven*ed fast. He lived fast and he died fast. But one great thing about Bronsky is that he didn't waste a second.

IF YOU'RE A TRUE ATHEIST YOU SHOULD BELIEVE IN GOD

I grew up in a home where God wasn't part of my upbringing. He was mentioned in moments of frustration like, "Oh, for God's sake!" Besides that, I was never asked to talk to God or believe in God. When I was a kid, I asked my mother if she believed in God and she told me, "Yes." That was the end of the God conversation.

Around my Bar *Mitzvah*, at thirteen, I had an epiphany. God doesn't exist. What is this God nonsense? Prove it to me. Where is God? I don't see God. Who is God? Why should I believe in Him? Why should I care? The questions grew and the answers were few and far between. No proof; no real reason why I should have any relationship with God. I decided that God was a lie.

Are you telling me that God, the creator and master of the universe, cares what I do? If there really is a God, He has a lot more to worry about than me.

Where did we come from then? A random occurrence of events. Something started it all and then it just evolved. Evolution. If someone really pushed me and I felt that, okay, there had to be something—some force that started the whole universe in motion—then I would say, "Call that God if you want." But from that point on, as far as I was concerned, there was no God.

That's how I felt until I was thirty years old. It took me a very long time to change my mind. I did it intentionally. I never really believed in God after my "epiphany" at thirteen. I thought there were people who were intellectually honest and then there were people that fooled themselves. We all *knew* there wasn't a God. Some people allowed themselves to have the wool pulled over their eyes and others were willing to look truth in the face.

As I grew older, I realized a few things. One is that some people really *do* believe in God, because for them God is real. For me He wasn't, but for them He was. The other thing I realized is that people who believe in God are much happier than those that don't. That really bothered me.

People who believe in God were like alcoholics and drug addicts, except their drug was Him. But God isn't a drug. God is a belief. Alcohol and cocaine are drugs. I looked at people who believe in God and saw that they were happier. They knew (not just believed, but *knew*) that God was looking out for them, wanting the best for them, and running the entire universe. Things didn't just happen randomly. Even though there was what we perceived as injustice in the world, God was good and just. We just couldn't understand everything He does.

Wow. Talk about a drug. God was the ultimate drug! I don't take drugs. I wasn't interested in the God drug either.

By twenty-one I was living a religious Jewish life without believing in God. Judaism is a funny religion. You don't need to believe in God to be Jewish. You just need to be born to a Jewish mother or have a kosher conversion. Judaism is a religion of mitzvot (commandments) given to the Jewish People by God.

I started keeping mitzvot because it felt good. It gave my life meaning, but I still didn't believe in God. I wasn't really sure what I believed in. I was happy with the outwardly religious life I was living. I felt a connection with something, but I didn't believe in a God that cared about me or that I could talk to and not feel like a hypocrite.

I had been married for five years. We had one child and another on the way. I was having lunch with a friend of mine who I went to university with. We were idealists and moved to Israel together. We would have lunch occasionally. He used to be religious and became an atheist. I was an atheist and was becoming religious. He asked me if I believed in God and, when I gave him some long, complicated answer, he looked at me, in shock, and said, "Wow. You *do* believe in God!" I could hardly believe it myself.

I looked at people who believed in God and told myself, if you're a true atheist, you should believe in God. As an atheist, I felt that I should be a "good person," living within the rules of society and living a life that made me feel good. If something made me feel good and it didn't break society's rules, I would do it. I came to the funny conclusion that if I believed in a God who listened to me and cared about me, and that would make me a happier person, then I should believe in God.

But what if I was wrong? What if there was no God? By then I'd be dead and wouldn't know the difference anyway. If there was a God, I would have lived a happier, more meaningful life and after I die something would happen. It was a win-win situation to believe in God.

After I had my "drug," I started developing my relationship with God. I felt like a hypocrite but, as I worked on my relationship, eventually I started seeing God in my life. I was living a religious Jewish life anyway, so when I brought God into the picture it was like adding sound to the movie.

When I allowed myself to believe in God, I gave myself a place to turn to for my problems and joys in life. Who do I thank when things go well in my life? God. Who do I turn to when I have problems I can't handle? God.

What is the advantage of not believing in God? Intellectual honesty? It just brought me frustration and sadness. However, when I have a source for my pain and happiness, I also know that everything that happens to me—good or bad—comes from the same God that created me. He also created me for a purpose. I'm not just some random blip in the universe. Everything has a purpose: the rock, the plant, the bird, the mountain, and me.

I tell God about my problems. I ask Him for help. I still have stress, but I know that any stress I have is simply a lack of faith in God. If everything is from God—the same God that created everything and is running the whole of existence every millisecond of the day—then what am I worried about?

For an atheist this sounds crazy. It used to sound crazy to me too, but the truth of the matter is that my life is much better since I started believing in God. The only thing I have to lose is intellectual honesty that won't matter when I'm dead. If I'm right, I will have lived a happier, calmer, more meaningful life.

ELI'S CHOICE

One of the reasons that I live in our neighborhood, Nachlaot, is because of the Machaneh Yehuda open air market, known as "the Shuk." I love to cook. The idea of living next to a fresh fruit and vegetable market made living in Nachlaot a dream come true. I end up going to the Shuk six days a week (it's closed on Saturdays). Since I'm there every day, I got to know the vendors. They recognize me, some by name, others by my face.

The stores in the Shuk come and go. The Shuk changes with the latest trends. Nowadays the trend is restaurants, but when the cheese stand first opened there fifteen years ago, it was something special. We keep kosher, and the selection of kosher cheeses was never very impressive until this new store opened up.

When I was growing up, I was allergic to all dairy products so I avoided them, even ice cream. I was given allergy shots growing up and now I don't have any allergies. I never liked cheese, except on pizza. I would cringe at the sight of any other cheese, even mozzarella that wasn't baked on a pizza. But when I got to Edinburgh (where I studied for my 3rd year of university), I decided to try cheddar cheese. I was hooked. When the new cheese stand in the Shuk opened up, I became a regular customer. I tried all kinds of new cheeses (most of which I didn't like) and got to know the vendors. One of them was named Eli.

He treated the store as if it was his own. One day I asked Eli if he was the owner. He blushed a little and laughed. "No," he said, "those days are over." Curious, I asked him what he meant. He said that he used to be a competitor to the current cheese stand. He sold stuffed vegetables, prepared salads and other delicacies. However, the owners of the new store wanted him out of business. They bought the store Eli rented for his business and raised the rent. Eli was forced to shut down. He owed so much money to the bank that they foreclosed on his house.

I asked Eli what he was doing there working at the store of the competitor that forced him out of business. He told me he had to make a living and this is all he knew how to do. So, he took the job.

I was amazed. How could he be so humble and accept such a defeat and then start working for his competitor? Not just that, but he was happy. He was always in a good mood; smiling, making jokes and downright jolly. How could that be?

He told me he had a heart attack from the pain of losing his business and his home. He realized that he had to make a decision: was he going to be depressed or happy? I was so amazed at this simple man. I asked him how he could be happy when just about anyone else would be depressed, and his answer changed my life. He told me, "Being depressed just makes things worse. It won't help me to be depressed or cry over what's already happened. I lost my business. I lost my home. I almost lost my life; enough already. I made a conscious decision to be happy and that's that."

Eli continued working at the cheese stand for about another year. He sold his house and had to move into a little apartment on the outskirts of the city. It did depress him a bit. I could see he wasn't the same Eli I always knew. Eventually he quit his job working for the competitor and opened a catering business that sold prepared foods to stores like the one he used to own. He just kept doing what he knew how to do.

Over the years, I've run into Eli in the Shuk. He no longer works there; he just comes around because he loves the market. He's always smiling. I saw him recently. He had a huge smile on his face. I asked him, "Eli, how are you doing, my friend?" and practically laughing with joy he said, "Everything is fine, thank God."

He shook my hand with his two hands and told me how happy he was to see me. Every now and then I remind Eli that he's my hero. "What are you talking about?" he'll ask me. I remind him how amazed I was at his decision to be happy no matter what the situation. He always says, "If it would make a difference, I'd be depressed, but since it doesn't, I choose to be happy."

YOU'LL FIGURE IT OUT
WHEN YOU GET THERE

Ever since the first time I attended a Boy Scout camp, I wanted to be on its staff. The Boy Scouts at home were great, but there was nothing like a Boy Scout "High Adventure" summer camp. They had outdoor programs like I had never experienced before: rock climbing on real mountain sides (not just climbing walls), white water rafting and kayaking, as well as backpacking trips with canoeing in the middle. Since I took to camp craft like a fish to water, I excelled at the Scout camps as well.

One summer my troop spent a week at Camp Daniel Boone in North Carolina. A couple of summers later, I joined their staff. The first summer I worked on the waterfront. The second summer I ran the rock climbing, white water rafting, and one- to two-week long backpacking trips. The previous summer I had worked at another Boy Scout camp in Wisconsin, also on the waterfront.

One of the first things I noticed—being one of the only Jews working at these camps—was people's reactions to Jews. Some people hated Jews, even though they'd never met one in their whole lives. Others loved Jews, even though they'd never met a Jew before meeting me. The hatred wasn't experiential hatred, it was inherited hatred. The kids that hated Jews didn't even know what a Jew was. They were taught that "Jew" should be used instead of some four letter curse word. I saw this more times than

I could remember. At some point I realized it wasn't Jew hatred, just ignorance.

There was one kid at the camp in Wisconsin who, when he jumped in the freezing cold lake water, screamed "Jew! Jew!" instead of an expletive. That was my first time hearing Jew used as a curse word. At first I didn't understand what I was hearing, but it got clearer and clearer every time this little kid yelled "Jew!" So, I made sure he ended up in one of my swimming classes and the next time he yelled "Jew" I asked him what he was doing. He was the one who explained to me that it was a curse word. His parents had told him to use Jew instead of the other ones.

"Why?" I asked. "Dunno, parents said to," was the answer. By the time the week was over, this kid and I were best friends. He knew more about Jews than most people and he could even sing the first line of the Israeli national anthem, *Hatikva*, in Hebrew.

He had an earring. The kid must have been thirteen years old, with an earring. He was a little bit of a spoiled punk. I joked with him all the time that I'd pull out the earring if he didn't take it off himself.

One day we were on the deck that extended from the shore to the lake. I was holding his earring, joking I'd pull it out, when this kid slipped and fell off the deck into the water. I was still holding his earring in my hand with a little blood on it. The kid and I were in shock at first, but then he started laughing. I apologized. He said his parents told him that if he came back from the camp wearing the earring he'd be in trouble, but if not, they would buy him some video game or something that he'd always wanted. He really wanted to remove the earring, but didn't have the guts. Now that it was gone, he was relieved, but needed a little medical attention.

My second summer in North Carolina, at Camp Daniel Boone,

I ran the long backpacking/canoeing trips, white water rafting and rock climbing expeditions. Since it was my first summer doing this, I had to learn the trails on the Appalachian Trail. There were a lot of them, and one wrong turn meant a dead end, a day late or worse. I had graduated high school and had more free time on my hands, so I asked to be hired as early as possible to help set up the camp for the coming summer.

Being in North Carolina, the camp had to be basically broken down and stored for the snowy winter. When I arrived early in the summer, I hardly recognized the camp I had known the summer before. The deck on the lake and the rafts were gone. The campgrounds were full of broken branches. Some of the bridges had broken over the winter.

For two weeks, every day, we labored in the hot sun piecing the camp back together. As the opening date for the camp arrived, the camp looked more and more like what I had remembered. I had driven my car from Miami to Canton, North Carolina where the camp was. It was hard to be at this camp without a car. It was literally in the middle of nowhere, which was kind of the point.

One morning after breakfast, the two senior staff members who had run the backpacking program for years were having a good laugh but were not letting me in on the joke. "What's going on, guys?" I asked.

"You'll see." This went on for a good half an hour until I couldn't take it anymore. "Go find your car," was the answer.

"*What?* What are you talking about? What happened to my car?"

"Nothing happened to your car, it's fine. Maybe just relocated."

I went outside to look for my car and it was gone. This camp was so remote and had a big locked gate at the entrance. There was no way my car was stolen. I found my friends and asked, "Where the hell is my car?"

They were laughing so hard they could hardly speak. "That's a great question. Let's go find it."

I still didn't understand what had happened. "Find it where?" I asked.

One of them pulled out a topographical map and pointed to a location about a hundred miles from where we were, "I think roundabouts here we parked it, right?" he said, looking at his friend.

"That looks about right," the other staff member agreed.

Now I understood what had happened. One of them told me, "Go pack up your gear for a two-week trip and meet us at our cabin."

The trail started from the camp. We walked to the edge of the camp and kept walking for two weeks. One of the first things I asked was for my car keys but they said they didn't have them.

"What are you talking about? Who has the keys?"

Laughing again, they said, "We hid them next to the car."

"Are you kidding me?" I wasn't happy about this at all. "What if someone steals the car?" They hadn't thought about that at the time, but assured me no one would find the keys, they were hidden well.

Many times during the two weeks we would stop at a certain fork in the trail. My guides would say, "Get out your notepad and make a note that when you're here, turn left." I'd look at the fork and tried to figure out how I'd ever remember that at this particular fork in the trail I should turn left. "How will I know?" I asked. "You'll figure that out. Make some notes, draw a picture, look for some sign so you'll know and write it down."

Sometimes I would move a large rock or break a big branch on a tree so, the next time I was there, I would remember which way to go. In a short time I would be guiding groups of thirty boys and their adult leaders through these two-week trips and, if I got lost, we would be in a lot of trouble. We had HAM radios that we could use in case of emergency, but I hoped it would never come to that.

Two weeks later we arrived at my car. It was full of bird poop and so many fallen pine needles I could hardly recognize it, but it was my car. One of the guys went into the brush and found my keys, hidden well, I have to admit, in a plastic bag. I opened the door. The smell of my car reminded me of home. We took it for an industrial strength cleaning.

A week later I took my first group out on the trail. They had no idea that this was my first time leading a group on a trip like this. I was an Eagle Scout and amongst the Boy Scouts, that means *a lot*. The adult leaders in our troop, all Vietnam veterans, used to give me the ultimate compliment, over and over, that they'd "follow me into battle." I was confident and experienced; I just hadn't walked these trails more than once before.

During those two weeks with the two senior staff members, we covered every trail and every variation of a trail that I might have guided that summer. If it was the one-week trip I would use this trail; the two-week trip that trail. There was also a canoeing section that we didn't even cover. "You'll figure it out when you get there," they told me. And I did, just not always in the right away.

I got lost on my first trip. It's a real dilemma to get lost with a group of thirty boys and their adult leaders. Do I say that I'm lost and lose their confidence in me, or just make a decision that I'm going to go left or right and hope I made the right choice?

I got to a fork in the trail and picked left instead of right, or maybe it was right instead of left? We were walking for about half a day when we came across a section in the trail that was marked with two long branches in an X. It clearly indicated that this trail was no longer safe or in use for some reason. However, it looked like every other place that I'd been. I imagined the rebellion I'd have on my hands if I told them I had taken the wrong turn at the fork in the trail. So, we kept going until we got to a part of the trail that had basically disappeared. The rain had eroded part of the trail and it fell into the valley below. There was no place to go but back. When I saw that, I turned around to the few boys who were staying up front with me and told them, "I made a mistake. We're going to have to go back." They were not happy.

Slowly the rest of the group caught up and everyone wanted to know why we had stopped. The adult leaders came one by one to the front. I showed them that the trail was gone and that, unfortunately, we'd have to go back. They were more angry than the kids. They threw all kinds of accusations at me, "How could you?" "You didn't know better?" "Don't you have a map?"

I had to stay calm and lead. I told the group to rest. Everyone should drink and eat something and then we would go back and walk as fast as possible so we would reach the clearing where we were going to camp for the night before the sun set. No one was happy with me, but we turned around and started walking at the quickest pace possible.

We made it back to the fork and went left instead of the right I took earlier. The boys and I made a clear marker with rocks saying the trail was closed and to turn left. We made a big arrow to the left. At least this made them feel good. We helped someone else avoid our own fate and maybe even saved someone's life. If they went on that trail at night, they might not have noticed that it was gone before it was too late.

There were two staff members with each group. One of us would take the front, the other the back. I reached the campground as the sun was setting, leaving an adult and some of the boys there and turning back to help with the slower part of the group. The staff member at the back was having a hard time. The kids in the back simply didn't want to walk anymore.

You had to be part coach and part therapist to get them to make it to the campground each day. I knew that, and headed back to take over for the other staff member. As I passed the other boys and their adult leaders they all said, "What? You messed up again?" I laughed and told them how far away they were from the campground. That in itself encouraged them to finish. "You're fifteen minutes away," I said.

I left some Oreo cookies back at the camp and made sure there was tea and hot cocoa so that, when the exhausted kids arrived, they would at least have some comfort. About half an hour from the camp, I ran into the second staff member. The Boy Scouts could take the worst kids and make them good, but take the best kids and make them outstanding. That was this boy. The sun had set and it was dark already. He had a flashlight hanging from the front of his backpack and was prodding the stranglers on. "Come on, guys," he said, with the biggest smile and all of the patience in the world, "You can do it. I know you can." He was relieved to see me.

"Barak. You're a sight for sore eyes. How much longer?" Then he confided in me that these kids had taken everything out of him and he could hardly keep going himself. I told him half an hour or less and that I would take over for him. Everyone said goodbye and I stayed with the slowest boys in the dark. They also seemed relieved to see me. It was a change of energy and they found the strength to finish. An hour later we showed up at the campground. Everyone was in a good mood.

I had to regain almost everyone's confidence the next day. We were going to be on the trail for a week together. The next morning I apologized to everyone before we started and promised it wouldn't happen again. Luckily for me, I never did get mixed up again. Not that summer or the summer after.

The second night, when everyone was settled in—tents pitched, dinner served, tired but happy—one of the adults called everyone together. He said, "We want to thank Barak for teaching us an important lesson yesterday." I didn't expect this. I figured, just move on and wait for the next group. "Barak taught us to know when you're wrong and not be afraid to admit it," he said, winking at me. It was also a lesson for me.

The staff usually alternated weeks on the trail. We worked in the "High Adventure" section of the camp which was kind of like the elite. We spent one week taking out a group on the trail, the next week "running the river," taking groups on white water rafting trips, and rock climbing for the day.

The white water rafting trips were run three times a day. We'd get up before sunrise and start heading out in a yellow school bus with the rafts on a trailer pulled behind. The ride to the river was about two hours from the camp. When we arrived we would take out the rafts, paddles and life preservers. While some of the staff inflated the rafts, the rest of us would give the orientation explaining what to do if you fell in the river, what to expect, and how to paddle.

I had grown up with a swimming pool in our backyard, and I took to the white water rafting like a fish thrown back in. I loved the thrill of it and learned to do all kinds of stupid things, like throwing myself out of the raft and swimming back to it in the rapids. It didn't always work out as planned. Sometimes another raft would have to pick me up and paddle quickly to the raft I abandoned so I could jump back in and take over. Sometimes the kids in the raft thought it was funny; sometimes they freaked out. I was really just a kid myself, having a good time.

There were parts of the river that most of the staff avoided because the rapids were too rough. That was the first place I headed with the same mixed results from my raft mates, some happy and laughing, some scared and crying. On the weeks when we weren't on the trail I could run the river three or four times a day, five days a week.

I always preferred running the river over the rock climbing trips. It was more action, less fear—at least for me. When I did my first rock climbing trip I was the junior staff member. The rock climbing was treated like open heart surgery. Everything had to be in place. All of the knots tied correctly, all of the gear checked again and again. There were backups on backups on backups in case something went wrong. We rappelled down the side of a huge cliff and then climbed back up.

On my first time rappelling down, I really didn't have any desire to climb back up. But the only way back up is to climb. I recall times when a staff member would have to rappel down to help talk a kid back up the cliff. At the end of the day, the kid had to get back up himself. I made my way back up and then took my position holding the safety, watching the boys as they climbed back up the cliff. It was boring compared to the white water rafting.

As we neared the end of the day, some of the staff members decided to race down the cliff "Aussie style," as they called it, face down and body forward. I guess it was called "Aussie," since Australia is on the opposite side of the world, meaning upside down. They ran down the cliff while holding on to the rappelling rope. We had four ropes set up, so four could race at a time. Watching it I thought this was the craziest thing I'd ever seen. By the end of the summer, I was one of the top competitors in the Aussie-style race.

This was the summer I fell in love for the first time and it was reciprocated. I'd had crushes before, but those girls weren't interested in me. Now I was nineteen years old and I'd found my self confidence. There were four women on staff that summer. All four were the most desired people at camp.

There were two Scottish women at the camp. They were foreign exchange staff. Both had boyfriends at the summer camp and I was just their friend. We became good friends and, as the conversations got deeper and deeper, a real love developed between me and one of them; Fiona. Even though she had a boyfriend, officially, all summer, I was really her boyfriend.

I'd never experienced anything like it before. Without realizing it, she changed my life. I guess that's how it is sometimes. We make decisions or have experiences that at the time don't seem like actual forks in the road, but whether we chose to go left or right can set the course for a person's entire life. Falling in love with Fiona led me to study for a year at the University of Edinburgh and put me on the path that led to where I am in my life today. Was it just meant to be or was it of my own free will? I'm not sure it really matters.

◆

I started playing the French Horn in 7th grade and by the time I got to high school I was playing the trumpet too. The Boy Scouts had a whole list of bugle calls. I took on the job of playing the bugle for my troop and also at the summer camps I worked at.

Camp Daniel Boone had a ceremony at the end of the summer. We lit a lakeside bonfire on the waterfront. There was an awards ceremony, some skits, and then it ended with me playing taps on my trumpet on a raft floating in the middle of the lake.

Playing taps in the dark for a few hundred boys at the final ceremony became a spiritual experience for me. People would tell me every week after I paddled back into the waterfront that something special happened when I played taps, and they couldn't explain it. It happened over and over again, week after week.

◆

We got paid in cash every week. I have no idea why they did this. It meant that we spent every penny of what we earned each week. Rare was the staff member who actually saved his money. It was too tempting to spend it on camping gear, food, beer or anything else we could find to spend money on.

By the end of the summer I had a top of the line backpack, custom fitted to my back as I bent over like when I'd be on the trail, the best boots, the best stove, the best of everything. The camping stores knew that, when the kids from the Boy Scout camp walked in, we'd spend almost everything we had.

One time, one of my cabin mates received a few dollars less than he was supposed to. "They Jewed me!" he shouted. I'd never heard this in my life.

"They what?" I asked.

"They Jewed me, man, they Jewed me." I had to ask my other friends what he was talking about and then they realized.

"Oh my God, Barak, I'm so sorry, I forgot you're Jewish." It was quite a revelation for me. My friends didn't hate Jews—we were the best of friends that summer—but someone down the line did.

I heard all kinds of variations of this during the summer. There were people that said they hated Jews but, when I asked them why, I could easily refute their claims. They said that the Jews run the media; the Jews own all of the banks; the Jews control everything. One by one I would show them that, if the Jews ran the media, how come the media was so biased against Israel? If the Jews owned all of the banks, how could Bill Gates and Warren Buffet be the wealthiest Americans? Jews, as a distinct ethnic group, are more successful than most others, especially minorities, but we didn't control everything.

◆

I don't know when I first heard the idea of having a calm place in your mind and going there when you need it. One of my calm places is a view from the top of one of the mountains on the Appalachian Trail, overlooking the other mountains. A cool wind is blowing and the sun is setting. My tent is pitched. Everyone in the group is fed and laughing. I'm calm, happy, content, exhausted and grateful. If ever I need to calm myself down, and I remember to do so, this is where I go.

The amazing thing about reaching the top of the mountain is that you can see all of the other mountains. It's never the end.

I stayed at the camp an extra two weeks to put everything away for the next summer. I didn't know at the time, but I would not go back to Camp Daniel Boone again, except in my mind. After those summers, life and the decisions that I made have taken me to greater and greater adventures. I can trace back the decisions I made that led me to where I am today to that last summer.

After everything was put away, I got into my car and started the drive up North to Rutgers College in New Jersey, where I was starting as a sophomore transfer student.

As soon as I closed the door, started the engine and the air conditioner went on, I understood the summer was over. I had avoided going in my car to cool off from the heat or to have some privacy but, now that the summer was over, there was nothing left for me at Camp Daniel Boone. The only choice was to move on; to move forward.

As I drove toward the front gate of the camp, I deliberately drove slowly, listening to the gravel under the wheels with the windows open. I passed through the gate and realized that this was a moment in time, in my life, that would never come back again. Even if I stayed in the camp until the next summer, everyone else would be gone. It wasn't the physical structure that made the place so special, it was the people in it. They were gone and the special moments were also gone. I took a deep breath, pressed on the gas, and moved the summer from the present into the past.

ONE DROP OF
WATER CONTAINS THE
WHOLE OCEAN

I went to visit my ninety-seven year old grandfather in Florida. It sounds cliché to have a grandfather in Florida, but he has lived there most of his life, so where else should he be? We spent real quality time together. That also sounds cliché, but when you visit once every three or four years, it has to be quality time or it's a waste. I asked him what he could teach me after living for so long. Was there one lesson in life he had learned after living fifty-four adult years more than me? He started telling me about how and where he grew up and trying to remember the lessons his own father had taught him.

He said that the family name was always important to him. People have to be able to trust you and know that, if you're a Bloom (his family name), you are honest and reliable. That wasn't what I was looking for and I told him so. I asked my grandfather to dig deep and think of a lesson he'd learned during his lifetime that could impact me and future generations to come.

He took on the challenge. He'd lost most of his vision and hearing, but his mind was all there. The next day we met again for the second and last time on my short visit (and, as it turned out, the last time I would see him; he died a few months later). This time he stepped up to the plate.

My grandfather said that he had been blessed with a lot of

money, power and influence. I don't know how much money my grandparents actually had. It was enough to get him meetings with big politicians, even the president of the United States. It certainly made him feel like a hot shot.

He was also the president of the National Plumbing Union in America which, for a plumber, is a huge deal. He and my grandmother donated many of the buildings in the synagogue we grew up in. He had scholarships and awards named after him. But his greatest pride and joy was serving as a first sergeant in the US Army in WWII and surviving the storming of Normandy. All of the money, power and influence were not as satisfying as that one small incident in WWII.

A few years ago, my grandfather made a speech in his Reform synagogue asking people to get more involved in Jewish life. He'd given this speech for sixty years, but no one ever seemed to listen. No one except for one couple who took it as the turning point in their lives. They decided to get involved in the synagogue and eventually became pillars of the community. The wife told my grandfather years later it was really thanks to him that they got involved at all.

My grandfather, with tears in his eyes, told me, "that meant more to me than all of the money, honor, power or influence I've had in my whole life. Someone saying you changed their life is worth more than all of the money in the world."

I often ask myself, what am I doing with my life? What impact am I having on the world? Very few people will ever impact the entire world for more than a generation or two. Most of us impact others on a seemingly small scale. Let's say I make someone's day by smiling and asking them sincerely how they are doing. Is that different than inventing the cure for smallpox?

Before looking it up just now, I had no idea who invented the cure for smallpox. It was Edward Jenner in 1796. This man changed the world. Smallpox could wipe out almost the entire population of the planet. Thanks to Mr. Jenner, we don't even think about smallpox anymore. That's a global, long-lasting impact, for sure. But when I make someone's day, who had more of an impact on their life? Me or the inventor of the cure for smallpox?

I'm a bit of a local celebrity and this is certainly not to brag. I lead the *davening* in one of the largest synagogues in Jerusalem that's not a yeshiva or a Chassidic sect. People come from all over the city and the world to *daven* in our shul on Friday night. Since I'm the prayer leader, many people recognize me, but I don't know them.

When the shul started getting popular, I didn't realize how many people knew me. The *shtender* (the podium where the prayer leader stands) in our shul is in the very front, which is the Chabad custom. So, when I'm leading the *davening* in front of three hundred or so people, I don't see any of them. They're all behind me.

As a result many of them know me, but I don't know them. In the earlier days, I would sometimes meet people on the street and they'd say "Hi" to me as if they'd known me for years. At first, I didn't say "Hi" back, figuring they'd mistaken me for someone else.

But eventually people started telling me that they had, in fact, known me for years, because they had been coming to my shul for years and *davening* with me, and yet I didn't know them. Of course, I was nice and had a short conversation with them. But then something else happened.

Someone approached me on the street and, instead of being

happy to see me, he was furious at me. He'd been *davening* at our shul for years and said "Hi" to me on the street, but I never acknowledged his existence. I apologized; I had no idea.

After that happened a few times, I decided that, any time someone even looks at me, I'll say "Hi" to them. For some people this is an easy task, but for me, even after more than ten years of doing this, it's not an easy thing to do. My personality can be outgoing, but inside I'm a total introvert.

Just before I get up to lead the *davening*, I'm very quiet. While leading the *davening*, I'm very extroverted. As soon as the *davening* is over, I'm quiet again. Saying "Hi" to strangers on the street is not fun for me, but having people think I'm arrogant is worse. So, I say "Hi" to a lot of people that I don't know.

Most of the time I'm right. The people who stare at me know me from shul, and want to see if *I* know them. When I say "Shalom" I can see they get excited. "You remember me?" they'll ask.

"Of course. I know you from shul, right?" I'll say.

"Yes. Wow. Thank you for noticing me!"

"How could I not?" I'll say, or something like that.

I became the *baal tefilah* (the prayer leader) many years ago when the shul fell apart. I took over responsibility for the shul and kept it going. I'm not a rabbi, but I played the role of rabbi for the congregation as we started to rebuild the community after it collapsed.

A year later we had a good crowd coming regularly. One day, one of the guys who had been *davening* there for the year came over to me for the first time. I knew his face, but didn't know his name. I did what I do with everyone who I recognize but don't know their names: I say, "Hi, I'm Barak. What's your name?"

He was a Conservative rabbi in training; finishing up his last year in rabbinical school. He told me that every Conservative rabbi in his class that year had been to my shul to learn from me. I had no idea.

"To learn what?" I asked.

"To learn how to build a community," was his answer. He continued, "We wanted to learn everything. How you greet people. How you lead the *davening*. How you speak to the congregation. You name it, we all learned from you."

One day I was in the elevator in my office building, heading to work. I walked into the elevator and there was a middle aged Israeli man there looking at me like he knows me. I wait a second and he's still looking at me. I say "Shalom" to him. He looks at me like I'm a little nuts.

"Do we know each other?" he asks.

I have a standard answer for that too since it has happened so many times. "No, but we do now. I'm Barak, what's your name?" This guy never told me his name. He just smiled, an excited smile. He was practically dancing in the elevator, jumping a little. When the next few people entered the elevator I learned why.

They came in. He was still dancing a little. The doors closed and he said to them, "This sweet man just said 'Shalom' to me. He doesn't even know me. And he said 'Shalom' to me!" He was so happy and excited he could hardly control himself. I shook his hand, saying, "We're good friends already." He was so excited, "Who says 'Shalom' to strangers these days? Thank you. Thank you! You made my day. You made my week. Thank you, friend." Luckily for me, I got out of the elevator on the next floor.

I realize now what I'm doing with my life. I'm changing other people's lives just by saying "Hello" to them. Sometimes I merit to do more, sometimes not even that much.

The Lubavitcher Rebbe said that one drop of water contains the whole ocean. All of the elements that make up the water in the ocean are found in a single drop of water. You might feel like you're not the ocean, just a little drop of water, but it's the drops of water that make the ocean into an ocean. Take away all of the drops and there would be no ocean. The impact you make on one person's life for one second of their life is like one drop of water. For that person it could be the whole ocean.

TURTLES ON THE BEACH AT NIGHT

When I was in high school I started jogging at nights. It's hot and humid in Miami. I tried once or twice to run during the heat of the daytime and, after realizing that I might die, I opted for the evenings instead.

I had a route around my neighborhood. My father gave me the idea to drive the route, measuring the distance with my car. I found a loop that was one mile long and ran that as many times as I could. I started with one loop and eventually I got up to running ten miles a night.

You can only run the same route so many times without getting bored. When the weather was nice I would go to the beach and run. We lived about a seven minute ride to the beach. There was a long boardwalk that went on for many miles. I would sometimes run on the boardwalk, sometimes on the sand. Sometimes I would go to a national park about twenty minutes from our house. It was a piece of beachfront preserved entirely in its natural state.

The forest led up to the beach, which sloped down quickly into the water. I would park my car and jog from one end of the beach to the other. The park was a few miles long in each direction. If I was feeling really foolish, I would run some of the way and swim some of the way. If, God forbid, something had happened to me in the water, no one would have known. There wasn't a soul anywhere at that time of night in such a remote location. That's what I loved about it, and that's also what was so dangerous about it.

Many times I would run with no shirt on, going in and out of the water. I loved the cool breeze from the ocean. I loved the solitude. It gave me a deep connection with nature. I enjoyed it so much that I went once a week for a while.

Sometimes I would see turtles or dolphins in the water. It was dark and there was only the moonlight reflecting off of the ocean. I was never sure if I was really seeing animals in the water or if it was my imagination. But one night, I was sure I saw eyes looking back at me from the water. I kept seeing them reflecting back the moonlight. As I continued running, I saw more and more eyes in the water. It looked like hundreds of them. They were all staring at the beach line and seemed to be getting closer and closer.

I continued running on the beach, constantly looking to the side to see if the eyes were still there. They were. There was no question now that I was seeing eyes in the water. Then I saw an ATV in the distance. I had never seen a vehicle on the beach in all of the months that I had been running there.

At first I was angry. What a chutzpah, I thought to myself. Then the ATV started driving toward me. As it got closer, I realized there was a state park ranger in it. I was sure he was going to tell me it's illegal to run on the beach at night, but what he told me took me entirely by surprise.

He asked if I had seen the eyes in the water. I thought he was joking at first, but then he said that those eyes were hundreds of turtles that were coming that night to lay their eggs and that there were poachers who would try to steal them. He told me to be on the lookout for anyone besides the two of us, and not to be surprised if I see the turtles on the land.

I kept running and the ranger went in the opposite direction. About five minutes later, I met the turtles. He told me not to be surprised, but I was. I stopped running. I knew right then and there that I was experiencing a once in a lifetime sight.

The turtles were slowly working their way up the steep slope of sand that connected the beach to the ocean. They hardly made any noise, except for the sound coming out of the water and sliding across the sand. Some were already on the land digging holes to bury their eggs. I stood there watching them in awe while they paid no attention to me. There was the light of the moon and the smell of the ocean; just me and the turtles. A few minutes later, the park ranger came back.

He told me he was going to stay there for as long as it took to watch the turtles bury their eggs and then stay until the morning to make sure no one took them. He told me I could stay as long as I wanted. We watched this miracle together until I realized it was getting late and my parents might be worried. There were no pay phones around. I started my jog back to the car, driving home that night in silence, not wanting to interrupt the awe made by the turtles on the beach.

THE PRIZE IS IN THE MIDDLE

Life is so hard sometimes; I hope there's a prize at the end. Some religions say there's heaven at the end; eternal love and goodness. That's not what I'm talking about. The thought I had was that, when you overcome all of your problems—when there's a moment that you do; *if* there's a moment that you do—what would the reward be? Peace of mind? Satisfaction?

I asked my grandfather before he passed away if he had any problems. By ninety-seven he had lived his entire life. Did he have problems still? Of course he did, plenty of them.

Maybe the prize is in the middle? The life you and I have led without even realizing it is actually the prize.

The prize is the "good times" we look back on which, at the time, we didn't recognize were truly good times. You might not have realized it at the time. Maybe all of the rewards we'd like are given to us slowly, piecemeal, and we don't even realize how much has been granted us? The awareness itself, that the middle could be the prize at the end, is the real prize.

ARE YOU AS HAPPY AS ME?

I have two friends who know how to be happy in life. Often-times I wonder why I can't be more like them. I'm always a lit-tle stressed and high strung, but these two friends, they know how to chill out.

One of my friends lives with his mother. He's thirty-five years old. He has a son and he's divorced. When I asked him recently about his business he said that things were going well. He told me he stops working every day at four o'clock. I asked him why he doesn't stay open longer. He said there's no need. He makes enough money working until four so, why work more?

When I was visiting him and his mother, he showed me a pic-ture of his son who just got into university. He was proud of his son. This is somebody who I'm not sure finished high school. It's a big deal for his son to go to university. He showed me his room in his mother's house. It was nice and clean. He even had a candle burning when he wasn't there. Then he showed me his pride and joy: his bicycle.

It's one of those bikes that you can lift up with your hand using one finger: superlight, superfast. I asked him how often he uses it and he said every day. He rides at least 70 miles a week. I thought to myself, how much more does a person need? He has a place to live where he'll never be kicked out. He has a business that makes enough money for him to live. His son is successful in his eyes, he has a clean and organized life and he even has a healthy hobby. What more could he ask for in life?

I have another friend. He's a little crazy. He's bipolar and, despite his mental disease, he was able to make it through Harvard medical school and become a doctor. For years he worked in emergency rooms in America and eventually he moved to Jerusalem. That's how we became friends. Over time, he went from being one of the most normal and balanced people I knew to being totally crazy and not even sure where he was. I haven't seen him since, but the last time I saw him he actually had some real words of wisdom for me.

I asked him how he was doing, and he told me he was doing great. He was standing in the middle of the Shuk drinking a beer, not looking so great, but certainly happy. I told him I was concerned about him. It was clear that he either wasn't taking his medication or that the medication he was taking wasn't doing the job.

And I'm sure that drinking beer wasn't helping. But when I asked him how he was doing, he said that he had his beer and his friends. He had clothes, food, and a roof over his head. What more could he ask for in life?

And then he said to me, "You know what, Barak, I'm actually concerned about you. How are *you* doing? Are you as happy as me? Can you tell me that you're as content as me, sitting here with my beer enjoying my life?"

It actually got me thinking: am I as happy as my crazy, drunk friend? It reminds me of the story you probably know, about the guy who is sitting by the lake fishing. Every day he catches a lot of fish. Eventually somebody who's been watching him comes over and says, "Why don't you sell that fish in the marketplace? You can keep some of the fish for yourself and the rest you'll make some money from."

So the guy who's fishing says to the other guy, "Then what?"

The other guy says, "Well, after you make a little bit of money you can hire some people and they'll also fish. Then you take the fish that you caught and the fish that they caught and you make a bigger profit."

And the guy who's fishing says, "And then what?"

"Well, then you buy a boat and catch even more fish."

"And then what?" asks the fisherman.

"Well, after that you buy some more boats and eventually build a factory and you make a fortune."

"And then what?" asks the fisherman.

"Well, then you have all the money you need."

"And then what?" asks the fisherman.

"Well, then you can do anything you want."

And the fishermen answers, "You mean like sitting here by the lake fishing?"

Sometimes life feels like a paradox. I work and struggle to make money so that I can have the freedom to do what I want. But maybe I really don't need so much money to do what I want? I've thought about my two friends many times. Why am I not like them? I've put myself in their shoes many times and tried to imagine what would it be like if I just had a room and a little business and rode my bike 70 miles a week, or had a beer and was just happy with what I had?

Some people aren't just happy to relax and appreciate what God has given them. Some people are like me and need more. We need to feel like we're part of something big and making an impact on the world. And people like me are really happiest when they're doing something. Every person is different and everyone has different needs. Every time I put myself in my friends' shoes I see how frustrated I get. But the thought of their happiness and serenity brings me comfort. Maybe one day I'll get there myself.

WALK SLOWLY

Do you know people who don't know how to slow down? They never have enough; running from one place to the next. It's the cause of stress and of success. Everyone knows the verse from *Pirkei Avot* (Ethics of Our Fathers) 4:1, "Who is rich? He who is happy with his lot."

I have many gifts from God, but there's one that allows me to appreciate the other gifts. It's the holy Sabbath; *Shabbos*. There's nothing like *Shabbos*. Everyone knows the famous story from the Talmud (Shabbat 119 a):

The Roman emperor said to Rabbi Yehoshua ben Chanina, "Why does the food [you Jews prepare for the Sabbath] smell so good?"

"We have a certain seasoning," replied the rabbi, "called the Sabbath, which we put into it, and that gives it the wonderful smell."

The emperor said, "Well, give us some of that seasoning."

Rabbi Yehoshua said, "[Sorry, I can't.] It only works for those who keep the Sabbath. If you don't keep the Sabbath, you can't enjoy it."

Shabbos is a time when we Jews separate ourselves from creation and just are. It's the ultimate time to enjoy what God has given us. One of the highlights of *Shabbos* for me is the midday meal. We start out with the nine of us, and then usually have five or six guests too. Toward the end of the meal, all kinds of friends stop by to join us. The meal usually lasts three hours or so. There's no rush. There's no place to go. It's time to just sit and enjoy. Just be. It's the highest, but it's only one day a week. What do you do during the rest of the week?

I have a trick that works for me. I walk slowly. I do everything slowly. I eat slowly. I look around me slowly as I walk slowly and, as I slow myself down, everything in my life slows down. It's kind of like a walking meditation with my eyes open. The goal is to be open to everything around me and to appreciate it. I try to focus on one thing and squeeze every drop out of it. If I'm eating something, I try to experience all of the flavors. If I'm smelling something, I try to smell every aspect of the fragrance. If there's something beautiful like wild flowers or a sunset, I try to embrace the moment, to stop everything, breathe deeply, take in everything, and appreciate it.

My thoughts will take me to all kinds of places. I end up appreciating my wife and sweet children, my tiny home, my clothes and my health. But it doesn't take long before I need to start walking again. Something pulls me out of my walking slowly. Sometimes it's something external; sometimes it's my own readiness to go faster. Whatever it is, whenever I get overwhelmed I know the secret of finding peace of mind. It's appreciating what I already have. It's walking slowly.

CHASING THE HURRICANE

When I was growing up in South Florida we went through a period of serious hurricanes. For years before, the hurricanes had been real, but not like they were then, which was much more severe. This occurred when I was in middle school. We all knew when a hurricane was coming, but we didn't know when it would get bad enough to have to leave school.

The whole school would be hanging out, watching the crazy weather outside, but school was still in session. All of the kids wanted to get out early. Every time there was a hurricane, there was always one kid that would get out of school early, and it was me. The other kids always knew it was just a matter of time before the announcement came over the loudspeakers for me to go the principal's office.

My father would be waiting for me outside of the school. We'd race down to Miami Beach where his optical store was to tape up the windows and put up the hurricane shutters.

Electric hurricane shutters back then were a rare luxury. The metal awnings over the store windows served as the hurricane shutters.

By the time we got to Miami Beach, the wind was so strong it could blow you over. The wind was blowing against my father's car as we drove over the bridge connecting Miami to Miami Beach. It actually made it hard to drive.

Once we reached his store, we taped up the windows in case the glass broke. It would at least keep the glass intact. Then we dropped down the metal awnings to cover up the taped windows. It was a whole process that would take a little more than an hour. There we were, father and son, in the crazy wind and rain, protecting the livelihood of our family and bonding at the same time.

The rain sprayed on and off and I loved the huge gusts of wind. The weather was cold, which was rare for South Florida. The wind blew the traffic lights around like they were mobiles hanging over a baby's crib. There were pieces of metal and garbage blowing down the street where the cars used to be.

After the store was shuttered up, we got back in my father's car and worked our way back home to North Miami Beach. Then we prepared the house for the storm. Miami Beach always took the brunt of the storm since it was a barrier island, naturally made for this purpose. Where we lived was a bit further in from the shore so the storm wasn't as bad by the time it reached us.

The day after the storm we headed back to Miami Beach to see the damage. Sometimes the traffic lights were on the ground, sometimes they were nowhere to be found.

Every time after the storm there were blown-over trees, broken glass, and garbage everywhere. It was clear that the storm had done its damage. Sometimes the store windows were broken and needed to be replaced. The store would be cleaned up and put back together. Life would go back to normal.

One time I came upstairs to my father's office and saw a piece of a traffic light. It was huge. I didn't realize they were so big. I asked him what it was doing in his office. He told me it blew off onto the street near the front window of the store and he took it upstairs as a memento. Then one day I noticed it was gone. My father told me, disappointedly, "The police chief came to visit me in my office the other day and saw it. He told me it was city property and took it away. What was I going to do with it anyway?"

It was never too long before they announced my name again over the loudspeaker. We would drive back down to Miami Beach while all of the traffic was heading in the opposite direction, chasing the hurricane.

There was a certain peacefulness about the storms. It was peaceful, exciting, and purposeful. My father needed me. My family needed me. There was no greater feeling as a kid than knowing you were doing something for your family that no one else would. All of the kids were jealous of me for leaving school early. But if they had known, they would have been jealous of the bond I was creating with my father and the feeling of satisfaction I had when we were driving away from the storm, our work completed.

A GUITAR, A VIOLIN, AND A DJEMBE DRUM

Life will humble you. This is a lesson I learned the hard way. For years I had the good fortune of having a web development contract with a major university in Israel. I got to work from home, didn't have anyone supervising my work, and made three times the average salary in Israel.

Israelis don't make that much, so three times the average is good, but certainly not great. It was more than enough money when we only had one kid, but by the time we had three it was pushing the limits. By the time we had seven we were sinking deeper into debt each month. I always had a business or two on the side, so I never lost hope. I went into debt always knowing that one of those businesses would pull me out eventually.

There were always signs that the contract with the university would end—it wasn't ever a real contract. They needed someone to do some web development fifteen years ago and I got the job. Then they said, "Hey, would you like some more work?" and I said, "Sure." This kept going on for fifteen years. There was a period of time when I was actually a salaried employee with no benefits and then back to being self-employed.

Each year, around October, the department I worked for would set their budget for the coming year. Every year I was told that I was being phased out or at least seriously reduced in my salary. I would get stressed and then at the last minute one of my co-workers would convince them to keep me on board.

This went on year in and year out until they actually did end the contract that never existed. They gave me two months' warning, but it wasn't nearly enough. Almost three years later I can tell you I needed about a two and a half years' warning.

Almost everyone struggles financially in Israel. Many people have left to go back to their birth countries because of this, hoping things will be easier. Every now and then the rabbi of my synagogue would ask me how I was doing and I would say, "Thank God, everything is fine." It wasn't great, but it was fine and, compared to most other people, it was great. He would say to me, "You have the contract with the university, right?" I'd nod. "Good, good, that's good," he'd say, and I would agree.

Then one day the contract ended, and at the same time my side businesses stopped making money. I did not know what to do. First my grandfather offered to help a little, but the money he gave us barely lasted two months. My parents helped a little and my in-laws paid our mortgage so we wouldn't lose our house. There were times when we didn't have food in the house; when my kids asked for a shekel to buy bubble gum, I literally did not have a shekel in my pocket to give them. The bank was constantly calling asking me what's going on and I defaulted on all of my credit cards.

Any ego I had up until that point was gone. I was humbled like I've never been humbled in my life. I always thought highly of myself. I went from a high school failure to a top student at Princeton; I was an Eagle Scout and always felt like I was a little better than other people. Now I was a wreck. I did my best to keep it together on the outside and sometimes on the inside. When close friends would ask me how I was doing I'd say I feel like I'm adrift in the ocean on a raft without a sail, rudder or paddle. God makes me go left; I go left. He makes me go right; I go right.

The truth is I never have much control over my life. It's just the illusion of control. The only choice I really have is between good and evil. I could choose to be happy or depressed. Most of the time, I chose to be depressed. In general, I'm a happy person, so the fact that I was depressed made me even more depressed.

Every year, during the festival of Chanukah, I light a large oil burning menorah in a public space near our house. I take out my guitar and play for an hour or so. Lots of tour groups come by and look at my menorah and hear me playing. It's one of my favorite times of the year. I love the cold weather and I love seeing people's faces when they see the menorah and hear the guitar.

But the year I lost my job, I could hardly muster the strength to even light the menorah. I usually light ten menorahs, but this year I only lit one. I didn't have the internal strength to go outside and play for the crowds.

On the fifth night of Chanukah, I walked to the Old City in Jerusalem and went to the Western Wall. I cried out to God to help me. After I had nothing left to say, I came home and went outside with my guitar. I told Hashem, "You can beat me, but I'll get up. I'm going to play the guitar even if it kills me."

I went outside and started playing. After about ten minutes one of the neighbors came out with a violin. I'd never met him before and he was an amazing violinist. Then someone came by with a djembe drum and joined us. Within half an hour we had another guitar player and two flutists. The tour groups came by and were greeted with a musical treat like I'd never seen in all the years I'd been doing this.

People came by and requested certain songs. Others sat with me and took pictures with their kids. Eventually I got tired and went back home. I felt like it was a turning point in my life and things had to get better. They didn't, but it felt good to have my spirits lifted.

I hoped that everything would improve after that night. The next three nights of Chanukah it rained, so I didn't go outside. I played the guitar at home instead.

It was hard for me to even walk to shul in the mornings. I told myself "Just take one more step." And then I would take another and another until I made it to shul.

My situation improved about six months ago. Just like my stability had suddenly ended three years before, it simply turned around again. I discovered a way of making money online that didn't even exist a year ago. The businesses that stopped making money when I lost my job all of a sudden started again. I work less than I used to and make more. Some of my debts have been paid off and my mortgage has been refinanced.

If the rabbi of my shul were to ask me how I'm doing, I'd have to say "Great, thank God." I still have problems, of course, and plenty of debt to pay off too. But one thing I don't have anymore is that little ego that made me think I was better than others. It's long gone. I left it on my raft floating in the middle of the ocean.

I BLESS JEWS ALL THE TIME

I lead the *davening* in a shul that brings together all kinds of interesting people. We're an orthodox Chabad shul that sings Carlebach melodies. That means almost everyone feels welcome and as a result people who would be uncomfortable or outcasts in other shuls come to ours.

There was a guy who showed up in shul one day. His name was Peter. He was tall and thin and reminded me of Abraham Lincoln. He seemed a little mentally slow, but very sweet. He was in his late forties or early fifties. He didn't look Jewish, but you never know.

Sometimes Christians show up with a kippah and hang out in shul for a while, then they disappear. Peter used to hang out in the back of the shul. I introduced myself to him the first time I saw him and we had a little superficial conversation. That's pretty much how it went for the first few *Shabbos*es I saw him in shul.

After we would have our short, awkward conversation, he would say to me, "Have a great rest of the *Shabbos*... good health... good family time... enjoy your meal... take care... good family time," always with a big smile. It was sweet, but strange.

He would say it slowly, like he had to think hard about what he was saying and what he was going to say next. I knew almost nothing about Peter. I never asked either. I only knew he was American because of his accent. Then one *Shabbos* he wasn't there and I haven't seen him since.

I didn't appreciate his sweet words until he was gone. I have no idea where he went or where he is. That was several years ago and

I still think about his blessings to me of "good family time." Now, thanks to Peter, I bless other people with "good family time."

Another character that used to visit our shul was Levy. We had actual conversations, so I know a lot more about him than I did about Peter. Levy was in his late sixties or early seventies when he first started coming to our shul.

He showed up one Friday night in the middle of an intense and energetic *davening* with two hundred plus people packed into the shul. He was a very small and thin man and had some type of stomach problem. Maybe it was Crohn's disease or something worse. He was from Russia and had a gold front tooth. We spoke in Hebrew. His Hebrew was very good, though not perfect and with a strong Russian accent.

That night Levy worked his way to the front of the shul and stood on the little *bima* (stage) in front of the aron kodesh (Holy Ark). With his back toward the dancing and singing congregation, he picked up his hands over his shoulders dramatically, like he was about to start conducting the shul. And then he did, waving his hands like a conductor with everyone singing and dancing in front of him.

We're all used to characters in the shul so, while we got a good laugh out of Levy, no one was very bothered by him. Then he turned around in the middle of the *davening* and blessed everyone with birchat HaCohanim (the priestly blessing reserved for Jews of the family of the high priests during the repetition of the shemonah esrey silent prayer).

At this point the rabbi lost his patience for Levy and told him to come down from the *bima*. Levy didn't care. He closed his eyes and kept going until he was finished. I, in the meantime, was up front trying to lead the congregation in prayer. I had to wait for Levy to finish before I could continue. When he was done he simply walked out of shul. Then the *davening* continued as before.

A few days later I ran into Levy on the street. He came over to me to tell me how much he enjoyed the *davening* on Friday night. I told him I loved having him in shul and that he should keep coming, but to save the priestly blessing for another time. He told me he blesses Jews everywhere he goes.

"Are you a Cohen?" I asked him.

"No," said Levy, innocently. I told him that only descendants of the high priests are supposed to give that blessing. "Nonsense," said Levy, "I bless Jews all the time. They need my blessings." I figured he was right and didn't bother arguing with him.

The next Friday night he showed up just like before. He made his way to the front of the packed shul, raised up his hands as high as they would reach, and started conducting us. This time I was prepared for Levy. I made him my new partner in leading the *davening*. I tried to pace the rhythm of the singing to his conducting. When he was done, he blessed us again with the priestly benediction. The rabbi really didn't have the patience for this, but I didn't mind.

When Levy came down, the rabbi asked him not to do that again and explained some halacha (Jewish law) about why he shouldn't be doing it. It was the last time he blessed us in the middle of *davening*. Levy would still bless us from the back of the shul or after *davening*, keeping his distance from the rabbi.

One time he walked in on the women's side. In Orthodox shuls men and women pray with a divider between them. Sometimes men come in from the women's side, not realizing. Levy, however, didn't care. He walked in on the women's side and saw Jews that needed to be blessed. He looked around quickly, picked up his hands and started blessing the women. I thought it was hysterical, but the rabbi didn't. When Levy finished, he came over to the men's side like nothing had happened.

I regularly ran into Levy on the street, usually in the Shuk, and we would talk. I learned that he had a daughter and grandchildren, from his non-Jewish wife from Russia. It upset him that his daughter and grandchildren were not Jewish because their mother wasn't. He kept in touch with her, but she was in Russia and didn't plan on coming to see him in Israel. He had no intention of ever leaving Israel again. "This is the Holy Land," he told me. "How could I ever leave?"

We spoke about his poor health. He told me that doctors don't know what they're talking about. That's why he was treating himself with eating the right foods. I warned him that he didn't look very good.

One day I ran into Levy on the street and he told me his health was getting worse. He couldn't really take care of himself like he used to. He said he needed someone to help him for a few hours a day at home, but couldn't afford it and didn't know what to do. I didn't have any experience with this. If I had the money, I would have paid for the help myself, but I didn't.

He told me there was an option for him to live in a government sponsored home in Netanya. I made a silly joke that it would take him a long time to walk to Jerusalem on *Shabbos* from Netanya.

A couple of weeks later he came to shul on Friday night and told me it was his last *Shabbos* in Jerusalem. On Sunday he was moving to the home in Netanya and probably wouldn't be back. This time he danced with us a little after conducting the congregation from the *bima*. He raised his hands in the air while going around the central *bima* with a mass of people singing and dancing. I made him a promise that night that I would continue raising my hands in the air on Friday nights after he was gone. I blessed him that he should be back soon in good health. It's been several years since Levy left and I haven't seen him since.

The Friday night after Levy moved, I realized it was now my turn to raise my hands in the air. I was so embarrassed that I could hardly lift my hands above my shoulders. It would be a process. I managed to lift my hands up to about the height of my ears—that was progress.

I did that for another couple of *Shabbos*es. The *davening* is different every *Shabbos*. I always push it as hard as I can, but don't always get the same energy back from the congregation. One *Shabbos*, not long after Levy left, we had an explosive, life-changing *davening*. It happens a few times a year.

It's like your soul is being lit on fire, in a good way, and you never want that warmth to leave you. It comforts you and gives you energy at the same time. It's pure, positive energy. At the peak of the *davening*, I couldn't help myself. I threw my arms in the air and started jumping up and down with my hands above me. It was amazing. Lifting my hands up like that released me from some type of anchor down here below. It raised me up and I never came down. It brought me to a new level.

I kept raising my hands in the air for many months afterward and soon realized other people were following me. They were also raising their hands in the air. You never know what will touch a person's soul and light them on fire. Not many people do it for me, but my friend Levy did.

DON'T YOU WANT TO LIVE LIFE A LITTLE ON THE EDGE?

During the summers that I worked at Camp Daniel Boone in North Carolina, we went on a shopping spree every weekend. We were paid in cash, had time to spare, and thought nothing about the money we made. There were some kids that really needed to save their money, but most of us blew it as fast as we made it. If you think about it, how crazy is it to give nineteen and twenty-year-old kids cash at the end of every weekend? You would have needed to be very disciplined not to spend the money. I certainly wasn't and neither were my friends.

Sunday would come, and we'd pile into my car. We had room for five and usually a sixth squeezed in somewhere. It took about an hour to drive into Asheville, the largest real city near the camp. After being stuck in a Boy Scout camp or spending a week or two on the Appalachian Trail, it was such a thrill to be in Asheville. For me it was more than just being in the "big city."

I actually really liked Asheville. I liked the people. It was a liberal refuge in the midst of "God's country," as the sign says when you come into North Carolina. There were several vegetarian restaurants and, being a vegetarian since age thirteen, I was in heaven. There were farmer's markets, tie dyed t-shirt stores, independent booksellers, and hippies everywhere. And there was a mall.

Growing up, there were white malls and black malls. One was next to where my father lived after my parents' divorce. It was once the preeminent "white" mall. It had upscale stores, a brand new movie theater, great restaurants, and even an old-fashioned merry go round. Kids would go out of their way to go there.

Not long after my father moved into the luxury building next door to the mall, it closed. It had been going downhill for years until eventually it made more business sense to shut it down rather than to keep the doors open. Eventually, it was sold and reopened, but this time as a "black" mall.

When my father's fancy building on the water was built, the mall was such an attraction that there was a walkway connecting his building to the mall. That way you could go to the great restaurants and movie theater without even leaving the building and being exposed to the elements. But eventually the walkway was shut down because it was bringing the "wrong kind of people" into the luxury building.

Walking into the mall, I was shocked to see how everything had changed. It was really run down. The pizza place was still there, but wasn't as good as it used to be. The fancy restaurants were replaced with fried chicken and more fried chicken. I figured the movie theater couldn't have changed that much, but I was wrong. It was run down too. The popcorn tasted like it had been made the day before and all of the movies were catered to a black audience. There were movies I didn't even know were in the movie theater. Of course, there were some blockbuster movies and I went to one of those.

The experience was actually different than going to a movie theater in a "white mall." The places in the movie where people laughed were different. There was a lot more talking. It was like being at a friend's house watching the movie rather than being at the movie theater. After the lights went on, I realized I was the only non-black in the theater; let alone the only visibly Jewish person. They were probably wondering what I was doing there.

As I walked out of the mall some people gave me looks that actually felt threatening. Some people even jumped at me as they walked by me to make me cringe and then laughed at their success. I didn't go back there again. It was better to ride my bike to Miami Beach where I felt more at home.

In Asheville the balance was different. It was clearly an old, run-down mall. There was a black guy with a boom box walking down the gallery. One of my white friends from camp, a self-proclaimed redneck, lunged at the black guy with the boom box and said, "Turn that thing down, boy, or I'll whip your nigger ass."

I don't know what shocked me more, what my friend said to this fellow or that the black guy actually turned down the volume on the boom box. If you had done that in downtown Miami where my father lived, you might be dead by now; either shot, stabbed or beaten by the guy with the boom box and his friends.

But not in North Carolina. There the blacks were scared of the whites. In Miami, the whites were scared of the blacks. I asked my friend what the hell he thought he was doing threatening the guy with the boom box? He told me simply, "If we don't keep them in their place, they'll take over like you probably have in Miami." I really didn't know how to answer him.

One Sunday, before we went to the movie theater, having calculated how much money I needed for the movies and some gas, we stopped at one of the hippie stores in Asheville. It was partly as a joke. It was full of crystals and African art and there were some colorful African hats. One of my friends put one on as a joke, but the saleswoman was ready to make some money and she convinced him to buy it. He told us to get one too. We were happy to try them on and laugh at how silly we looked.

Then somehow these hats turned into a bonding experience. We were all going to come back to camp with these hats; a sign of the good times we'd had together and the brotherhood we would have in the future.

I reluctantly picked out the hat that I eventually bought, picking the hat that would stand out the least. I wasn't so excited by this whole idea.

The owner of the store who had now joined the saleswoman came over to me and said, "Why the most subdued one?"

"What?" I asked.

"Why are you taking the most subdued one? Don't you want to live life a little on the edge?"

Actually, no. I didn't. I just wanted to waste my money on this hat that I didn't really want and get to the movies.

The hat served its purpose. When we got back to camp everyone was jealous of the good times we'd had and the brotherhood we shared, but not of the ugly hats.

The hat is long gone. I never wore it again after that summer, but the question has stayed with me ever since. Why the subdued one? Don't you want to live life a little on the edge? The real answer was, oh, yes, I do. I'm just too scared of what others will think of me.

That hat probably cost me ten dollars or so back then, but the question the store owner asked me has been priceless. "Why the subdued one?" I would ask myself, Is that the woman I really want to date? Why go for the one I think I can get? Why the subdued one? Go for the one you think you can't get and live life on the edge. Should I start the business that's easy and will probably work, or the one that's crazy and that I really want to do? Should I live where it's safe, or where I really want to be? Should I, should I, should I? I ask myself often, "Why the subdued one?" Why did I make that decision? Is that really what I want? And that question has given me a glorious life so far. It has taken me to places and to people that would never have been a part of my life had I not been so eager to waste money on a silly hat.

ELI IN THE WINDOW

I live in an interesting neighborhood full of interesting people. When I first moved here, I lived on Shirizli street in Nachlaot. Our neighbor was Eli Cohen (not the famous spy). He lived in a small, old house (our neighborhood is about 130 years old), made of Jerusalem stone. It has a window facing the pedestrian street with old iron bars that extend outward.

When I first moved to Jerusalem, these bars made an impression on me. We didn't have any bars on our windows when I was growing up in North Miami Beach. We had an alarm system. Here they have iron bars and it makes sense. They're cheap and efficient, unless you have to get out the window because of a fire, God forbid. Then you have a little problem. I didn't want bars on the windows of our house, but my wife said if we didn't have them we'd be the number one target for thieves.

Our neighbor Eli would sit perched in his window on a big old pillow and talk with the passersby. He grew up in Iraq so he spoke fluent Arabic. He always conversed with the Arab street workers in Arabic and the Jews in Hebrew. His English was also okay.

One of the things he would say when he started his first conversation with you was that he was Prime Minister Menachem Begin's driver.

This was a loaded statement. You didn't become Menachem Begin's driver because you were a nice guy or a good driver. Before he was the Prime Minister of the State of Israel, Begin was the head of the Jewish underground that forced the British out of Mandate

Palestine (pre-state Israel). He was brilliant, strong, passionate and, most of all, valued loyalty.

Everyone around him as Prime Minister was connected to him through their pre-state activities. So, if you were his driver, it meant you had done some serious stuff in the Jewish underground and that Begin trusted you with his life. Eli told me there were some close calls. He wasn't just a regular driver. He knew "evasive maneuvers" and sometimes had to use them.

When they pass by a nice, old smiling man on his pillow in the window, most people stop and start a conversation. Eli was like a street vendor waiting for his next customer. Sometimes he had two or three people talking with him, but he always made sure to say to me, "Shalom, Barak."

This is what I called "paying the Eli Tax." I would just walk out of my house, turn right to go to the Shuk and there was Eli. Boom, at least ten minutes were gone. Sometimes they were interesting for me, but always they were interesting for Eli.

Eli always complained about how hard it is to be old. He looked old. He'd been through a lot in his life: moving from Iraq, resettling in an underdeveloped, dirt poor Israel, fighting for his life and for the survival of the state of Israel against the British and then against the Arabs. Life had taken its toll on him.

A few years later Eli passed away of old age. He was seventy-two. I was sure he was in his mid eighties. A person can age themselves, but it might also be life's circumstances that age a person. A lot of pain and suffering can certainly take its toll. I don't know everything Eli went through. As far as I know he never married and didn't have any kids.

I still pass by Eli's window every day. The apartment was sold and renovated. I'll bet the people renting there now have no idea how special their window is. When I pass by Eli's perch I can still see him leaning on his pillow talking with the passersby. I used to find it annoying to have to pay the "Eli tax," especially when I was in a rush. Now I pay it voluntarily when I stand in front of Eli's window and remember my old friend.

I'M NOT READY TO GET MARRIED YET

I know so many people who are waiting for certain circumstances to align before they do all kinds of things: get married, buy a house, start a business, go on a trip, have kids, make an investment, or live their life dream. I totally understand them. I was exactly the same way. The only difference is that I didn't listen, and did these things anyway.

When I was seventeen I came to Israel on a high school program. I was in Israel for two months. After I came back to the States, I realized how much I loved life in Israel and decided I was going to move there. But I didn't really know what that meant or how to do it. By the time I was eighteen, I decided I was just going to love Israel from America, but never talked about moving there again.

I would come back and visit as often as I could, which was once a year in the summers. I did that until I graduated from university at twenty-two. Then I was free to go anywhere I wanted as long as I could fund it, and the only place I really wanted to go was Israel. I ended up on a kibbutz for a year.

After dreaming for years of getting into Princeton University, I finally did and went back to the States to study for my Masters in Arabic and Islamic Studies. While there, I was introduced to a professor from the Hebrew University of Jerusalem, Professor Yohanan Friedmann.

He offered me a full scholarship, a grant and a job at the Hebrew

University if I would come back with him the next year to continue my graduate studies. I was a bit torn.

Once in Jerusalem, I was set up as the editor of the Islamic studies journal at the Hebrew University: *Jerusalem Studies in Arabic and Islam*. I had an office and even a secretary, as well as a salary. I never needed to pay for my degree all of the years I was at the Hebrew University.

Twice a year I would get a notice to come to the grants office and pick up my check. Sometimes it was $10,000, sometimes $500, but there was always something there for me. It was pretty amazing and I didn't really appreciate it at the time.

From practically the first day I landed in Jerusalem, Professor Friedmann who recruited me from Princeton was prodding me to get married. He'd point out women in the hallways and say, "What about that one?" When he finally saw me with the girlfriend that eventually became my wife, he nagged me every day to marry her. But I wasn't ready. The truth is that, even after I was married, I wasn't ready to get married.

Three weeks after starting to date my wife, she said to me, "We're getting married, right?" We were speaking in Hebrew at the time. She's a native Israeli. I'd say I understood about seventy percent of what she said, the rest I kind of figured out by the context. When I realized what she told me, I broke off the relationship. I wasn't ready to get married and I didn't want to waste her time. She was devastated and didn't understand what had happened.

A few days later we were back together with a promise that we would just date for a while before talking about marriage. But she was just waiting for me to come around. After six months, she said we had to get engaged. "Okay," I said, "we'll get engaged." We did.

We had a nice little party in South Florida. I didn't realize at the time that my grandfather wouldn't live to witness the wedding and my other grandparents would feel the trip to Jerusalem was too hard to make.

About six months later, Noga, my wife, said we had to get married. I agreed to plan the wedding, but I told myself I could cancel at any time. I wasn't ready to get married.

We planned the cheapest wedding we could. We were too lazy to look at wedding halls. There was a new one under a plastic tent in the parking lot of a yeshiva near the Hebrew University. We picked that one. We'd go for "food tastings" and free dinners every few nights. It was a free date with a good meal. Right up until the day of the wedding, I wasn't ready to get married.

Three years after being married, Noga told me we have to have kids. "Kids?" I cried, "I'm still not ready to get married!" But I realized that she was right. What's the big deal? I asked myself. We'll have a kid or two. No problem. I figured kids were a good thing. They'll take care of you when you get old. It's like an insurance policy—I had no idea what I was talking about.

Our first child came, and then within twelve years we had seven kids. Around ten years after being married, I told my wife that I was ready to get married now, but certainly not ready to have kids. She was pregnant with our sixth at the time.

After our firstborn came home with us, my mother-in-law started nagging us to buy a house. I've had a lot of ups and downs with my livelihood. Back then I was making ends meet, but had almost nothing saved up for buying a house. And I certainly wasn't ready for the commitment of a mortgage.

Then my great uncle passed away. He never had kids. He was

successful in business and made a little money, leaving a bit to most of his relatives and a large sum to one of us. I got the little bit, which came in stock—I'd never traded stocks before. This was at the start of the tech bubble in 1998. After I traded the electric company stock my uncle left me for Yahoo and was making $500 a day, I thought I was a genius.

We started looking at homes. We only wanted to live in a very special, old neighborhood in Jerusalem. We were very specific and even knew which streets we wanted to live on. That's when Nachlaot, our neighborhood, was still a slum in transition. There were drug dealers and pimps and prostitutes on the streets. I knew them all, even by their first names. We found a house we wanted to buy but couldn't afford it even with my in-laws helping us out. I certainly wasn't going to sell my stocks. I was living off of the income.

We found the perfect house, but it didn't work out. When the negotiations fell through, I was a little devastated. Then the stock market crashed. I lost over $20,000 in a day. I had taken the little inheritance my uncle left in stocks and turned it into over $300,000. I was able to take a few thousand dollars a month out of my investments and pay my bills.

I tried to short a stock as the prices were dropping but no one would buy my short. I attempted to sell a stock that I owned, but no one would buy that either. I was just watching the money disappear in freefall. It was sickening. Just then we found a house. The price had dropped from previous years. I felt that prices would keep dropping and maybe the stock market would recover and I'd make my fortune back.

My mother-in-law was practically screaming at me to sell my stocks and buy a house right away before prices went back up. My wife said that my mother-in-law knew real estate, but I was a hot-shot trader. I knew markets, and the Jerusalem real estate market wasn't cheap enough for me yet. As I watched my fortune disappear by the hour, I lost any confidence I had in buying a house.

My wife told me to sell everything that was left of the stocks, about $20,000 at that point, and to use it towards the down payment on the house. I sold all of my stocks. It was a devastating moment for me, as I wasn't ready to get out of trading.

"What if the market recovers tomorrow?" I'd ask my wife. Then I realized that, for the first time in my life, I was addicted to gambling. I couldn't believe it. I'm a straight arrow; an Eagle Scout. I don't enjoy gambling, drinking, porn or even sports. And here I was addicted to gambling in the stock market. It stunned me.

The Buddha said, "The problem is that you think you have time." If it were up to me, I'd still be figuring out if I was ready to get married. Look at how much I would have missed out on. How many times do opportunities come, and we let them pass us by while we're trying to figure out if we're making the right decision?

When you're waiting for your luggage at the airport, do you ever take someone else's luggage intentionally? Someone might have beautiful, designer luggage that has seen the world. We always take our own luggage. We want our underwear and our shoes. We might like someone else's, but our luggage was made for us and their luggage was made for them.

I know that my problems were custom-made for me. When I find myself jealous of someone else, I imagine the conveyor belt at the airport and choosing to take my luggage and no one else's.

Fortunately, I ignored my inner voice. I did what logically

seemed right, even though I wasn't ready for it at the time. And that has made all the difference.

ONLY PEASANTS DRINK SOUP FROM A BOWL

My grandfather was a character. My father's father grew up in Lithuania and moved to America at ten years old to escape the pogroms against the Jews. He was one of seven children.

My great grandfather was an old school Orthodox rabbi who immigrated to Elyria, Ohio from Lithuania. I have a few letters that he wrote to my grandfather which he left me after he passed away. Two of them are in very poor English. In one, he begs my grandfather to let him write in Yiddish, because he didn't know English well enough to express himself. My grandfather refused to speak Yiddish, even though he grew up in a Yiddish speaking home.

In the letter, my great-grandfather describes how it's getting harder and harder to go down to the basement and slaughter the chickens. He kept the Jewish ritual of eating only kosher even though he was an old man and it wasn't easy for him. Since there was no kosher food where he lived, he raised and slaughtered his own chickens.

My grandfather wanted nothing to do with that life. When he was a kid the non-Jewish kids in his town would cut the *eruv* just before *Shabbos* so the Jews couldn't carry on the holy Sabbath.

When I would drink soup from a bowl my grandfather would yell at me to stop. "Only peasants drink soup from a bowl!" I didn't know anything about peasants growing up in North Miami Beach.

I drank from a bowl because it was easier than using a spoon. But for my grandfather it represented something totally different.

My great-grandfather sent my grandfather to public school in Ohio. There weren't any Jewish schools there. He showed up with *peyos* (sidelocks), a *yarmulke* (head covering) and tziztios (strings worn under your shirt).

The kids there had never seen anything like it. They taunted my grandfather for the funny way he looked and his odd Yiddish accent. He didn't speak English and that certainly didn't help either. It didn't take long for the *yarmulke* and *tzitzios* to end up in the garbage and for the *peyos* to be cut off. My grandfather was going to be an American. Americans played football, which became an obsession for my grandfather, all the way up to playing a year for Ohio State University.

He tried many businesses over the years. None of them made much money. He read a lot and was an intelligent man, but financial success eluded him. He invested in stocks, collected coins and had a huge collection. It was kept in the mattress of the fold-up bed in the "den."

My grandfather told me that he had cash hidden in the house. He hid it in emptied-out cans of dog food in the back of the pantry. At some point, he drew me a map of the cash. I was sworn to secrecy but eventually I told my father about the hidden cash. He rolled his eyes. My grandfather had been doing the same thing since my father was a teenager. He asked me if my grandfather showed me the same dog food can with the cash. He did. Still, a secret was a secret and I now knew where the cash was, "just in case anything happened."

Coupons were a second religion for my grandfather. We would

drive around town chasing deals, going to Nathan's for hotdogs and then McDonalds for french fries. We couldn't have the french fries at Nathan's because there was a coupon for McDonalds. Forget about the gas wasted driving between the two; a coupon was a coupon.

We had a swimming pool in our backyard and my grandfather's greatest joy in life was pushing my brother and me into the pool with our clothes on. He also loved Christmas, even though we didn't celebrate it. He said that Christmas was an American holiday, and he was American.

He would never give us Chanukah presents. He wanted to give us Christmas presents instead. My mother was not happy about this. After a couple of times ignoring my mother's requests to not give us Christmas presents, we were forbidden from going to my grandparent's house on the day before or after Christmas. For sure, not on the actual day itself.

A new plan was called for. He celebrated Christmas a week early. There was a tree with our presents underneath. There was even Christmas music playing in the background.

My grandmother had worked for my father in his optical store since he started the business. I once found a name tag in the store for a "Mrs. Smith." When I asked my father who that was, he said he used to call my grandmother "Mrs. Smith" in the store so no one would think she was his mother. But when my father realized how much people liked him having his mother working for him, she went back to being Mrs. Hullman.

Eventually, my grandfather started working for my father too. I had worked there with my father and grandmother for years, but now my grandfather was also in the store. It was a pleasure for me and one of the great times of my life, working with my grandparents. We became very close.

My grandfather didn't like most people, unless they were rich and white. We had a lot of religious Jews come into my father's store on Miami Beach. My grandfather looked down on them, especially the ones that tried to speak with him in Yiddish.

He hated the Cubans and the Blacks even more. I realized he was a bigot. When I told him so his reply was, "Are you saying I hate Blacks more than Cubans?"

I shrugged my shoulders, "Maybe..."

"No," he said, "I hate them all equally!"

A lot of old people came into the store on Miami Beach. Whenever someone over ninety would come in, my grandfather would ask them what was their secret to a long life. One drank hot water with a squeeze of lemon; another took long walks every day. I'd always ask him after an old age interrogation what he learned. "It's all nonsense," he said to me. "They don't have a secret."

My grandfather died at eighty-five. He never made it to his own interrogation of how he lived to ninety-plus. I begged my grandfather before he passed away to have a Jewish burial and to be buried in the ground. Even though he was happy that I had embraced my Judaism and was living a religious life, he wanted to be cremated. My grandmother, father and aunt made sure his final wishes were carried out.

A couple of days after my grandfather had passed away, I went to take something out of the trunk of my father's car. There was a little plastic filing box there that I'd never seen before. I had a feeling I knew what it was, but wasn't sure until I asked my father.

"Did you open it?" my father asked me.

"No, of course not."

"Good," he said, "that's your grandfather."

I had a feeling it was him in there, but I couldn't believe that a person could be reduced to so little. You can't sum up a person's entire life in a few pages, but you can put him cremated into a little plastic box.

"What are you going to do with him?" I asked my father.

"I don't know yet," he said. "He's going to stay in the trunk for now."

Eventually, my grandfather's ashes were sprinkled over the grave of my great-grandmother, his mother-in-law, so that my grandmother could visit the burial site of her mother and husband at the same time. They were smuggled into the Jewish cemetery at night, since you aren't allowed to take human ashes in there. And just like that, my grandfather was gone. A whole life of eccentricities and philosophies disappeared into the wind.

WHAT IS THAT NAIL THINKING?

While *davening* in shul on Friday night, I found a nail on the wall and focused on it. I had the thought, *what is that nail thinking?*

He probably thinks: *I'm awesome. I'm made of metal. I've been hammered into a cement wall. I've been here for years, invincible. What could ever possibly happen to me? And I'm important. People hang their coats on me. They hang the calendar on me. I'm strong. I'm reliable. Everyone needs me and I have a great view. I can see the whole shul. Ah, to be a nail on the wall... that's the good life.*

But what would happen if one day, just because that's how things happen sometimes, maybe because of so many people using the nail, he falls out of the wall? It'll happen when no one is paying attention. One day he's on top of the world, the next day he's laying on the floor.

"Oh, how far have I fallen?" the nail sobs. "What has become of my life? I had everything. I *was* everything. And now look at me. Oy vey! My life is ruined."

What's the floor thinking now? *Finally, that nail has fallen. How many years did he sit up there, full of pride, thinking he was so important? Telling me and the others how he was strong, invincible, how he could see everything from his penthouse, how nothing could break him. Now look at that pathetic nail, laying on his back on me.*

If it weren't for me, he'd fall forever.

"You see, you bragger," the floor says to the nail. "You'd better thank God for me. If it weren't for me, you'd have no one to fall on. How far could you possibly go with a *floor* underneath you? Never underestimate the power of a floor, you foolish nail. I'll never fall out of the wall. I'll be here forever. This building couldn't exist without me. Ah, to be a floor, now that's the ultimate."

The whole night passes with the nail on the floor crying over his loss. Then the next day and the day after that. No one even notices that the nail has fallen. And, oh, how far he has fallen. The nail doesn't know what to do with himself. "How will I ever get back up there to where I once was?" he asks himself. And he knows, with certainty, that he cannot raise himself up without help. Nonetheless, he tries.

Almost an entire week passes. The nail is still on the floor. It's Friday afternoon, the guy who arranges the shul is cleaning the floor and arranging the chairs. He sees the nail on the floor, picks it up and looks up to find where it came from. He sees the hole in the wall where the nail used to be. The nail stops crying while he's being picked up. "Finally?" he says to himself. The guy presses the nail back in the wall and walks away.

As he clears his tears the nail realizes he's back in the wall, back up in the penthouse, but he could fall back out any second. "What?" he says to himself. "I'm hanging here by the skin of my teeth! I could fall out and be right back to where I was in an instant. What will be with my life? What will be with me? Oy vey."

How much stress can a nail experience? He's getting a migraine. He thinks, *Okay, this is better than being on the floor. I mean, how low can you go? A floor? That's pretty bad. At least I'm not a floor!*

But this instability is killing me. It's making me insane. I can't stand the stress of living life on the edge.

The nail realizes there's nothing he can do. He's back, kind of. He can't wiggle himself deeper into the hole. He tries, but after all he's just a nail. Self conscious, but inanimate. Then, he sees the cleaning guy coming back... with a hammer.

"Could it be?" the nail says to himself, "Maybe that hammer is for me?" But before the guy comes to the nail, he goes to *another* nail and pounds *him* into the wall. "Another nail?" he screams in agony. "Why him and not me? What? I don't need saving? I don't need to be hammered into the wall? I need stability! My God, have some compassion on me. Please."

Then the guy comes over to our friend, the nail, and grabs him at the sides, really tight. He hits him hard on the head with the hammer. The nail lets out a bitter scream, "You are killing me. Oy! The pain." Then he's hit again, this time harder than before, "Oh my God. Stop it! I can't take the pain anymore."

But the cleaning guy doesn't speak Nail, he speaks English, and hits the nail again, hard, again and again. The nail feels like this pain will never end. "Will this be my life now?" he says to himself. "Is this my destiny? A life of pain." And just then, the cleaning guy stops, checks the nail, and walks away.

The nail opens his eyes. He couldn't bear to see the hammer as it was coming to hit him again and again. "Is it over?" he says, still feeling the sting of the blows. He feels the stability of the wall. He's deep in the wall and secure.

It's just like the good old days. No, even better than the good old days. He's so strong into the wall, could he ever fall out again? "This is awesome," he says to himself. "I did it. I made it. I'm invincible again. I'm the king of this wall. No one will ever knock me down again."

The floor looks up at the wall. "Don't be so impressed with yourself, nail. You didn't do anything. All you did was complain. You cried. You wailed. You screamed. You were stressed out of your mind. You think you actually *did* something? You didn't *do* anything. All you did was be a nail and you didn't even do such a great job of that. What kind of nail are you?"

The nail was about to make some snide comment to the floor like *Who are you to talk? Everyone walks all over you.* But then he realized that the floor is right. Yes, he's a nail, but outside of being born a nail and having the fate of a nail—which is to be hammered into something—what did he really do? And when the test of his life came, when he finally could do something, what did he do? *Total meltdown.*

The truth is his life has never been so good. But he knows the floor is right. Just because he was a strong, reliable, invincible nail high up on the wall, it was nothing to brag about.

The nail has been humbled and it feels real. For the first time in his life, he gains perspective, maybe even some wisdom. He hopes never to fall from such heights again. But if he does, he knows—at least he hopes—that next time he will be stronger than before.

"ASSAM ALAIKUM" (POISON UNTO YOU)

When I was eighteen I decided to give my life some real direction. I had tried to before but, after graduating high school, it was different. All of my friends had left to start their lives either at universities or in the military, while I remained behind. I was determined to get my act together.

It hadn't been so bad when I was a failure in high school. But after I was rejected from every university that I applied to and seriously considered whether I wanted to join the military, getting my life in order became my number one goal. I started by registering for community college.

I was going to give myself the education that I never got in school. I went to the bookstore and bought over four hundred dollars of Penguin Classics: history, philosophy, religion and science. I started with the first book and by the end of the year had read them all.

I really didn't know what was going to become of me after high school. I was literally the only person amongst the group of friends I grew up with who was still at home, not sure what to do with his life. Both of my parents owned businesses. They both offered for me to work for them and eventually to take over one of the businesses, but, to be honest, neither of them seemed happy with their chosen careers. I thought to myself, why would I want to be as miserable as them? I'm going to get as far away from here as I can.

I had a dream of going to Princeton. I knew nothing about Princeton except that it was in the Ivy League and it sounded prestigious.

I started working hard. My plan was to get a 4.0 in my first semester and apply to the University of Florida as soon as possible. I had friends that went there. I drove up to visit them and it looked so much better than the life I had. I was determined to get there as fast as possible.

Focused like a magnifying glass, I was trying to light a fire—my own fire. I read every book and article assigned. Then I read related material that wasn't assigned. I wrote my papers within a day or two and handed them in early.

Math had always been a problem for me. I have some numbers dyslexia. When I moved to Jerusalem, I would get on the 23 bus only to discover—when it was going in the wrong direction—that I was on the 32 bus. This happened to me so often that I started asking the driver what bus I was on. It even happened when I knew it was going to happen. Regardless, I was determined to at least pass algebra.

I knew that math worked in logical stages. As long as I understood each preceding stage, I would be able to understand the next. I took every class one step at a time. If I didn't understand something, I would ask the teacher to explain it until I got it. I started to love math, though I never took another math course again.

After the first semester with a 4.0, I was admitted to Phi Theta Kappa, the honor society of two-year colleges. Five months before, I had barely graduated high school. Now, I was in the national honor society.

It was a special time in my life. I was mentally calm, running every night and in better physical shape than any other time. I was working in my father's office making eyeglasses in the lab, having turned my life around. But this was just the runway. I was ready to take off and conquer the world, so I started applying for universities.

First I applied to the University of Florida. The amazing thing was, after I got a 4.0 in my first semester of community college, the University of Florida rejected me. They would only accept me after I finished a full two years of community college and received my Associates degree. I was flabbergasted. I figured that, if I was a good student, I could get into just about any university. The truth was that I could, just out of the state of Florida.

I was accepted into Rutgers, the University of Chicago, Fordham and was put on a waiting list for NYU, which eventually accepted me. It was amazing to me how my life had turned around in such a short amount of time. It wasn't just hard work that did it, but having a specific goal with a clear path of how to get there. I understand in retrospect why these universities accepted me, but at the time it was like an academic rags to riches story.

I chose to go to Rutgers. I knew almost nothing about Rutgers except that it was founded ten years before the United States in 1766. That made enough of an impression for me. I was a French Horn major in community college, but realized after one semester of playing in the local orchestra that this was not what I wanted to do in life.

After my high school program in Israel, I thought I wanted to study Jewish History, or maybe Middle Eastern studies. I wasn't sure. Every school I applied to had both programs, so I could change my mind after I was there.

Rutgers was a huge university. I thought I was going to a small, elite college—which it was—but as part of a larger university system. Just about everyone was from New Jersey. Students asked each other where they lived by saying "Which exit?" meaning, which exit off of the New Jersey turnpike are you from? When I told them I was from Florida, they freaked out. "What, are you out of your mind? You left Florida for the 'armpit of America'?"

The campus became a ghost town on the weekends. Often I'd be the only student around. All of a sudden it became very lonely. I had gone from being a king in community college to being a tree in the forest at Rutgers. I was so lonely that I told my parents I was thinking of coming back home.

My father came up to visit me. He stayed in a hotel near the university and said he'd stay there until I told him to go, or we went back together. My father would make these grand statements, hoping that it wouldn't come to that. If it stretched him too far though, he'd say enough is enough.

He stayed for a few days. I needed his companionship and had to make another decision. Now that I was where I wanted to be, could I find my place? I sent my father home after a few days and promised I would stay at Rutgers for the whole first semester. If I didn't like it, I would then apply for the University of Florida.

I went to a psychologist on campus. It was a free service provided by the university. I told him how lonely I was and he put me in touch with an out-of-state students counselor. I didn't even know such a thing existed. This woman was full of energy. As soon as I walked into her office, she told me the solution to my problem.

"Join every campus group you can." I was required to attend an out-of-state students' orientation meeting, but I didn't go. She told me no one had showed up to the first meeting, so she was doing it again and we all had to be present. It was scheduled for two weeks from the initial meeting.

During those two weeks, I joined every single group I could. I had no problems academically and was even more motivated than I was in community college. It was like one big adrenaline rush; I felt unstoppable. I finished my first semester at Rutgers with a 4.0. Socially, I suffered, until I started joining the groups.

There was a student center where almost all of the groups met. On the wall of the student center was a list of groups and their meeting times. Every single weeknight I went to the student center and spent two or three hours attending two or three different group meetings.

I went to the anti-abortion group and, the next hour, to the pro-life group. I joined the Zionist group and then the newly founded Muslim society. I joined the capitalist group and the socialist group. I started meeting people, learned so much and was no longer lonely. By the time I attended the out-of-state students meeting, I was telling other students how to find friends and integrate.

Three groups that I joined stood out for me more than the others: the Film Society, the Muslim Students Association, and the Zionist group. I always loved movies, so joining a group where we watched them seemed like a good idea.

As soon as I joined, Joe, the head of the Film Society and a fellow Jew from Miami, made me the assistant head of the society. I told him I didn't want to be the assistant. I was too busy. "I'll pay you twenty bucks a week to be my assistant." That worked.

He told me that we decided which movies the society would see, received the movies when they arrived at the university, and collected the money. The university would pay for any movie we ordered, so we picked every major motion picture we could.

Well over a hundred students would attended each showing. We charged five dollars admission. There would easily be five hundred dollars in the till by the time the movie started and Joe would tell me to watch the cash while he ran up to run the projectors. Then, once the movie was running, he put the money in an envelope to be given to the university and took twenty dollars out of his wallet to pay me. He did this every week.

After the first semester, Joe decided that I was now the head of the Film Society. "What? Wait! Me? I don't want to be the head," but Joe thought it was because I was afraid of not being paid. "Don't worry, I don't pay you out of my own pocket. That's just because I knew you wouldn't take the money if I gave it to you from the till. Take as much cash as you need. I pay myself every week from the till. You're in charge now. Have fun."

The first week, I handed over all of the money to the university. I continued doing this for the rest of the year. But the truth was, I didn't even want this job in the first place. Eventually, I hired someone to take over for me, paying him from the proceeds from the movies, just like Joe did for me, since he also didn't want the job.

I decided very quickly to major in Middle Eastern Studies rather than Jewish History. I planned to study specifically the Palestinian-Israeli conflict. As part of my own personal education, I joined the Muslim Students Association.

They were founded the year that I began attending Rutgers and I loved it, though my Zionist friends were worried for my life. There was one guy who took Middle Eastern classes with me, a Christian convert to Islam who chose the name "Jihad" (holy war against non-Muslims). He didn't want me to be at the meetings because

I wasn't a Muslim. Everyone else knew that was against university policy, but Jihad didn't care and made his discontent clear to me.

The customary greeting amongst Muslims is "assalam alaikum" (peace be unto you) which is just like in Hebrew "shalom aley-chem." However, Islam teaches that if you're talking to an infidel, you don't say "assalam alaikum" but rather "assam alaikum" (poison unto you). Every time I would say "peace unto you" to brother Jihad, he would answer me with "poison unto you" drawing out the "s" sound in poison (assssam).

At that first meeting, they needed twenty student signatures to officially start the group on campus. I was twentieth since there were only twenty students there. I attended the meetings the rest of the year and learned a lot, especially about how much they hated Jews. They had no problem making anti-Jewish comments right in front of my face. They figured if I had decided to come, it was my problem. After enough complaints and a recording of one of the meetings given to the university administration, they toned down the anti-Jewish talks, unless I missed a meeting.

The Zionist group was the funniest of them all. There was plenty of anti-Israel hatred on campus and we had no clue how to deal with it—the first time I'd encountered the problem. I grew up in a section of South Florida that was so Jewish, it seemed like everyone was pro-Israel, but not at Rutgers.

I once went with my Arabic class to a barbeque at our teacher's house. On the car ride over (in my car), someone mentioned how much they hated Zionists. I said, "Why? I'm a Zionist." The whole car couldn't believe it. They kept telling me that I was too nice of a person to be a Zionist.

When I told them that Zionism was the national liberation

movement of the Jewish people, they told me I had no idea what I was talking about. Zionism was, to them, Jews treating Palestinians like the Nazis treated the Jews. The Zionist Group spent the year trying to combat Israel-hatred on campus, but I don't think it made any difference other than making us all closer.

One day, one of the leaders of the Zionist group decided that we all had to make *aliyah* (immigrate to Israel). I was planning on making *aliyah* regardless, so I supported him. One night, he said we had to plaster the campus with posters that said, "Aliyah is the Answer."

I helped him put the posters all over campus. On a university bus at one point, someone asked what "*aliyah*" meant. We were putting up all these posters and no one even knew what we were talking about. It was really a silly thing to do, but it was fun. That's what students do: things that they think are cool, but are usually stupid.

All of that wasn't enough for me though. I also started writing for the student newspaper. I joined the outdoors club and started whitewater kayaking and, on the weekends, I discovered Chabad and Hillel; Jewish organizations working on campus.

Everything turned around. I had good friends at Swarthmore College nearby and started going there on weekends. I didn't need to call on my father to visit me again, even though he did sometimes. He would tell me he needed the vacation. I never knew if I should believe him or not.

My second year, I went to study at the University of Edinburgh in Scotland. When I came back to Rutgers, it wasn't too big for me anymore. It was just right.

It just goes to show you the power of intention, focus and applying yourself. I'm now much older than I was back then, but these were anchors in my life. These experiences molded me into the adult I am today.

When I was in high school, I was called into the school counselor's office. He looked at my grades and said, "Do you like Burger King?"

I told him, "No, I don't eat fast food and I'm a vegetarian."

Looking at me over his reading glasses he said, "Well, you'll be working there soon with grades like these."

I asked him why I needed to go to college. "Plenty of people are successful without college," I retorted.

"True," he said, "but many people look back at their college years as the best years of their life. Do you really want to miss out on that?"

As I'm writing this, I can say that he was right.

NOW DON'T LET YOUR HEAD COME DOWN

While working at Camp Daniel Boone, I became friends with Kim, the only female staff member that ran backpacking trips with us. We were just starting to become friends when, one morning at the flag raising, she turned to me and said in Hebrew "*Shema yisrael adonai eloheinu adonai echad*" (Listen Jew, know that God is everything and everything is God), which is the most basic prayer that virtually every Jew knows. Since I was the only Jew on staff, I was amazed when I heard her say these Hebrew words to me.

Kim told me that her father was a minister and in her church they learned and followed many Jewish traditions. We became good friends. When the summer ended, she told me to visit her at Swarthmore College where she would be starting as a freshman. One of the ways I got through my lonely first year at Rutgers was visiting Kim and her friend Emma at Swarthmore.

I became a regular visitor at Swarthmore. I'd come early on Friday afternoon and leave Sunday night or Monday morning. It was the best of both worlds. I was treated like a student at one of the elite colleges in the country without having any of the responsibilities or expenses.

I couldn't get enough of the atmosphere and the students. The grounds were beautiful. But it was the feeling of "this is where I belong" that kept me coming. I'd never even heard of Swarthmore before visiting my friend and I never saw myself as an intellectual or a snob, but this whole campus was full of intellectuals and snobs and I loved it.

The students at Swarthmore thought of themselves as the best of the best. I went to a movie on campus with Kim and Emma. The parents in the movie were bragging to their friends about how their son *and* their daughter both got into Harvard. The crowd of students started laughing. "Harvard sucks!" They threw crumpled up paper and soda cans at the screen while booing. "I chose Swarthmore over Harvard!" one student shouted.

For me, Harvard always seemed like the best you could get, and yet here I was amongst friends who made fun of Harvard. Having been an academic failure, rejected from every university I applied to after high school, I felt like I had been rocketed to the moon. Not only was I amongst this group, but I was accepted by them as a peer. It did more for my self esteem than I could have imagined.

I would come back to Rutgers and feel like I was smarter than almost everyone. I would take on my professors in class, feeling like I belonged to the elite, and they appreciated it.

My friendship with Emma became more than just a friendship. This was at the time when my Scottish girlfriend, Fiona, was travelling around the world. She broke up with me and I deepened my relationship with Emma.

Eventually Emma wanted to visit me at Rutgers, but I tried to avoid it as much as possible. I had nothing to hide at Rutgers; I just liked being at Swarthmore so much that I didn't want to leave.

◆

One day when I got off the train at Swarthmore, this attractive woman came over to me and said, "Ben, you're an asshole." Then she walked away in disgust. I had no idea what just happened. My friends had to figure out who this Ben was. They started asking around. It didn't take long to find someone who knew Ben and told us that we looked so much alike I could have been his twin brother.

That Friday night I went to the Hillel Jewish services on campus. It was a small group, maybe five people. I walked in and right away someone said, "Ben. I can't believe you came!" Then she realized that I wasn't Ben and practically screamed. "You look just like him."

Within a short amount of time, Ben and I were brought together. We both agreed that we looked nothing like each other. Then he himself said, "Okay, you look a lot like me." I asked, what's with the girl that called me an asshole earlier that day. "Seriously?" Ben asked. "That was my ex-girlfriend. She hates my guts. But you can date her if you want. She'll probably like you." As I got to know Ben a little better, I understood why the ex didn't like him so much.

◆

Eventually I started driving to Swarthmore instead of taking the train. My friends didn't have a car. We'd eat in restaurants off campus, go to concerts in Philadelphia, and run the occasional errand. Over those years, everyone always commented on my car, saying they had spiritual experiences driving with me.

When I worked at the Boy Scout camp near Asheville, we would drive into town and then back to camp late at night. I like to listen to relaxing music. I'd usually put everyone in the car to sleep by the time we got back to camp. But sometimes my friends would wake up while I was listening to, for example, Peter Gabriel's "Don't Give Up," and not say a word.

I would be driving and something would happen. I can't really explain it, but we could all feel it. When we got out of the car at camp, we'd look at each other and ask, "Did you feel that?" Yes, we all felt it, but could only explain it as a spiritual experience, not knowing what really happened to us. The same thing happened with my friends at Swarthmore. We'd be driving late at night with my music on and, after we'd get out of the car, they'd ask if we all felt it. It got to the point that my friends would invite an uninitiated friend to come driving with me late at night to feel it.

◆

Things with Emma and I were always intense, but on a low burner. I went to study in Edinburgh the next year, but we agreed to keep in touch via email. I learned about email because of my friends at Swarthmore.

"Do you have email?" they asked me.

"What is email?" I asked. They explained it like this.

"It's like sending a letter in the mail, but it's free." I thought it was a joke and couldn't wrap my head around the concept.

"Okay," I said, "so you write a letter and then put your address on it, but how is it sent for free? You don't need to put a stamp on the envelope?"

"No," they'd say, "you don't get it. You don't write on paper. You write on the computer and send it via the computer."

"Okay," I said, "so how do you get it?"

"We have an email address. You send it to our email address." I still didn't understand.

"Send it from where? How does my computer know to send it to your computer?" There was something missing.

"Oh," they said, "you need an email account. When you get back to Rutgers, go the computer farm and ask for one."

After going to the computer lab, I got an email account and an internet account. Back then there were no visual browsers, just a text-based Lynx browser. You'd type in a number which would give you a menu. Then you'd type in another number and end up in some university library somewhere where you could search part of the catalog online. It was pretty mind-blowing back then. But when visual browsers came out, that really blew me away. Without realizing it at the time, I was witnessing the start of the public Internet we all use today.

I kept in touch with Emma while I was in Scotland, but by the time I came back to Rutgers for my last year, we were just friends. At that point I was keeping the Jewish Sabbath and didn't drive from Friday sunset until Saturday sunset. Emma would borrow my car on Saturdays. She asked me if it was the same car we had the spiritual experiences in. When I told her it was, she treated it with such respect, but never had any more spiritual experiences in it.

Looking back, these memories of Swarthmore became an anchor in time for me. Time can be a great memory filter, sifting out the bad and leaving the good. I try to only remember the good anyway. It wasn't just an anchor in time; it helped me define who I was and who I am. I still see myself as worthy of being in a crowd I originally felt I had no right to be a part of.

I realize now, in retrospect, a lot of who we become in life is dependent on how others see us but, even more so, how we see ourselves. See yourself as worthy of something lofty, and you will be. Even if you don't actually get there, it will still raise you up to a place you wouldn't have reached otherwise.

When I was in the marching band, the band teacher taught us how to stand up straight. He said, "Stand on your tippy toes. Now come back down, but keep your head in the same place. Don't let your head come down." After we'd all do that, he'd say, "Now stay there." That's what Swarthmore did for me. It raised me up and I've told myself ever since, "Now stay there."

I FELL INTO A PIT

The other day I fell into a pit; not metaphorically. I actually fell into a pit dug by Arab workers in front of my house. The pit was over six feet deep. I know, because I'm 5' 11" and I was literally in over my head. The workers had to pull me out of the pit, injured and really upset.

I came home with a trolley full of food from the Shuk and, to my utter surprise, found that the pedestrian street where I live had been torn up. The stairs were gone and there was a huge tractor blocking the way to get into my house.

I looked at the workers and said, "What the hell is this?"

"Go around," they told me.

"I can't go around. I live right here," I said, pointing to my door.

"No problem," they said, "you jump over the pit into your court-yard, and we'll hand you your groceries. By the end of the day, the pit will be filled in and you can leave your house."

I wasn't happy about this at all. I don't jump over pits. Maybe when I was a kid, but not as an adult. But they didn't give me a choice. So I climbed up onto the mound of dirt and mud which covered what used to be the stairs to my house. I wanted to prepare to jump, but promptly slid into the pit instead.

Within half a second I was standing, injured, in this huge pit. I yelled at the workers that they were idiots and tried to get out on my own. It was too deep and full of wet mud. They had to pull me out. My leg had already swollen so much I could hardly walk.

I opened the door to my house, cursing out the workers and still in shock at what had just happened. I was so angry that I told my wife never to let me get a gun because I would have shot the workers if I had one. I wouldn't really have shot them, but I was so angry at what happened I felt like I could hardly control myself. Eventually my foot swelled so much that I couldn't keep my shoe on.

I know what you're thinking: I could sue. Forget about a lawsuit. I live in Jerusalem; it would be an endless battle against the city, and nothing would come of it. That's part of the cost of living here. Sometimes it's good, sometimes bad. I was exhausted and went to sleep.

A few hours later, I had to go to my office to work. I looked outside and nothing had changed. I was determined to get to my office, so I jumped over the pit with my good leg and then, with the workers helping me, I was back on the street again.

I limped toward work, wanting to treat my injured self to a nice meal. There was a fish restaurant that I hadn't been to in a while. It wasn't too far from my office, so I limped my way over. It sounds crazy, but that's how I am. I do stupid things like this. When I finally got there, to my shock and dismay, I saw that the restaurant was gone, replaced by another.

What the hell? I said to myself. Really? What else could go wrong today? Now I was really upset. I had fallen into a stupid pit, then I had dragged my injured self for some comfort food and the restaurant was gone. Having no other option, I started limping back to my office.

I recalled a lesson from Rebbe Nachman that I've given over many times at our *Shabbos* table. He said, "You have to love the bad things that come your way." Love the troubles and afflictions that come your way, because they are *your* troubles and afflictions, custom-made for you, to help you grow and become a better person.

Rebbe Nachman said that you have to accept them "with love." What a concept. I decided it was time to walk my walk and said out loud, "Hashem, I accept being thrown into the pit with love."

I kept repeating it out loud. Not too loud (I didn't want people to think I was crazy), but loud enough for it to sink in. "I accept my troubles and afflictions with love. Thank you, God, for throwing me into a pit! Thank you, God, for my swollen leg and foot."

Somehow, I'm not really sure how, I released my anger toward the workers. I saw them over the next few days and really didn't hold a grudge against them. The more I started to think about it, I thought, who threw me into that pit? It wasn't the workers. Yes, they were negligent, not covering the pit or taking any precautions, but they didn't throw me into the pit. Hashem threw me into the pit. He's also the one who pulled me out. The same God that put me in the pit, took me out.

JUST PAINT WHAT YOU SEE

I spent a couple of summers as a camper at Interlochen in Michigan. It's a world famous music and art camp, which made a huge impact on me. When I was accepted, I thought I was a great musician.

You had to audition to get into the camp. I played the French Horn at the time, made tape recordings of my playing and sent them off the camp with a recommendation from my music teacher.

When I got in, the teacher and I were ecstatic. I flew up to Michigan from Miami to attend. On the first day at the music camp, we had to audition for which orchestra we would play in. I was given a piece of music to play, but could hardly play it. "No problem," said the dismayed judges, "try this," giving me something simpler. This kept going until they finally ended the torture; mine and theirs. They placed me in the last position in the lowest level orchestra.

I was shocked. I thought I was an amazing French Horn player. In my little high school in North Miami Beach, I was. But here, with budding world class musicians, I wasn't.

I called my parents, teary-eyed, begging them for private lessons on the French Horn. The judges at the audition told me that my only hope was private lessons. I overheard them asking themselves how I could ever have gotten accepted to this prestigious camp. My parents couldn't afford the camp, let alone private lessons. But the camp gave a little discount, and my parents dug deeper to help out their son.

I was blessed with a teacher who really believed in me. He made me his personal mission that summer. One week I decided I was going to become the number one French Horn player in the lowest level orchestra, or even better, the lowest ranked French Horn player in the highest level orchestra. I practiced day and night.

Each week there was a competition where each player would challenge the player ahead of them. The other players would vote who played the passage better, and either the player would keep their seat or lose it to the player below them.

When the challenge came, I beat out the player ahead of me. She was stunned and embarrassed, but also a little happy for me. We had been at the bottom together for weeks. She never saw me as a threat but, now that she had lost, she was on my side, cheering me on to make it further up the line—and I did.

I beat out the next player and the next, until I actually beat the number one player and became First French Horn in the lowest orchestra. Everyone was shocked. The teacher that coached us all was blown away. He was literally speechless. The previous first horn player was so upset he could hardly muster the ability to say "Congratulations."

Now I had an opportunity to compete against the last horn player in the higher orchestra. After I beat him, I became the lowest French Horn player in the highest level orchestra, but I missed all of my friends from the lower orchestra. The next week, I didn't feel the motivation to keep my spot and everyone was relieved to see me last again. I was too; I wasn't made to be a French Horn player.

This camp took itself very seriously. You had to have a major and minor concentration, like in university. I majored in French

Horn and minored in painting. I had never painted in my life. I was so fortunate, however. The painting teacher was an angel. He was passionate and loved teaching.

It was a totally different atmosphere than the cut-throat competition of the French Horn. In the art classes I was told, "Just paint." When I had no idea how to paint, the teacher said, "Just paint what you see."

He put a fire extinguisher in the middle of the room and took some other random items from the art studio, then told us, "Paint what you see." When I told him that I didn't know how to paint what I see, he told me not to look at what I see in front of me, rather look at what I want to see. "Don't look at the fire extinguisher, look at the shadows it makes, look at how the light reflects off of the metal, look at the different colors and shades of colors you see, and then paint that."

So, I did and, all of sudden, I discovered I knew how to paint. I was just painting what I saw, and somehow it came out beautiful. I spent much more time painting than playing the French Horn.

This teacher was so wonderful. He would come into my area of the studio, see what I was doing and say with smiling enthusiasm, "Do more! Just paint! We won't run out of materials. Paint as much as you want, as long as you want. Please, do more!" What a difference from what I was supposed to be doing that summer, playing the French Horn.

Besides being one of the kindest and most supportive people in my short life at the time, this teacher taught me a very important lesson on how to be present. He taught me how to look at things. Instead of seeing the clouds, look at the shadows they make. Look at the shades of colors. When you look at your children or spouse, or anything else in your life, look at it like a painter would, and you'll be present in ways you never imagined existed.

EHDIN-BRA LIKE A WOMAN'S BRRRA

As soon as I got to Rutgers, I started applying to study at the University of Edinburgh to spend the year with Fiona. I went into the overseas administration office to enquire.

"Maybe China?" the administrator said excitedly. He was jumping around the room, pulling out brochures, telling me to go to this country or that one.

"Edinburgh," I calmly told him.

He looked at me for a minute and said, "Wait, Scotland? Why Edinburgh? How about Glasgow, or St. Andrews?" with a twinkle in his eye.

Shaking my head, "Edinburgh, that's it."

Fiona had decided to travel around the world for the year. I received letters from different countries and sent packages ahead of where she would be next.

Every few weeks, we'd talk on the phone. Everything was going great. I would talk with her mother back in Scotland on the phone. She told me little gems like, "I never had anything against the Jews," and other interesting thoughts.

About six months before I was to leave for Edinburgh I stopped getting letters from Fiona. She was now in Australia, renting a room with a kind, older woman called Harriet. I called and asked to speak with Fiona. Harriet said she wasn't in.

I tried again the next day and the next. Sometimes I called and she was sleeping; other times she had already left the house. Eventually I got a hold of her and Fiona told me she had met someone else in Australia.

She didn't mean for it to happen, but it did, and she was in love with someone else. She asked if I was still coming to Edinburgh.

My head was spinning. I called the next day; Harriet answered and told me that Fiona had left the house already.

Harriet told me something I'll never forget. "Let the bird out of the cage. If she comes back to you, she's yours. If she doesn't, she never was." Then I called Fiona's mother in Edinburgh who I had spoken with regularly. I could hear the relief in her voice. She said to, "Keep your chin up." I was heartbroken and registered and paid for a year at the University of Edinburgh.

I called my father. "You're going," he said, not realizing that he had always dreamed of going to Scotland and now I was his best reason to visit. When I asked him why, he said: "It can be a stepping stone to take you places you never would have gone without it. You're registered. It's paid for. Just go and make the most of it."

I arrived in Edinburgh by train, taking a taxi from the train station to the Kenneth Mackenzie International House (Ken-Mac House for short), my home for the year. I knocked on the door of the house, and this nice old Scottish woman answered.

"Hi," I said, "I'm here to study for the year at the University of Edinburgh," and I pronounced it Eeden-berg. The woman called for her husband. This nice old man in overalls looked me up and down, and then started cursing like I'd never heard in my life.

Since I couldn't understand his accent, I didn't really understand the curses, but they were definitely curses. I told him what I told his wife, "Hi, I'm here to study at the University of Eeden-berg."

"Oh, bloody hell, man," he yells at me, "it's not Eeden-berg. It's

Ehdin-bra, like a woman's brrra!" drawing out the rolling "r." "Get your bags and go over to the car."

I had spent that summer in basic training in the Israeli Army. Following orders was second nature by now. Within a few seconds, my bags were in the car and I was sitting next to the nice old, potty-mouthed man, driving me up the hill to the International House.

He told me this happened every year. It's the same number and street name, only that one is at the bottom of the hill and the other at the top. He knew I would have to hire a taxi to take me up the hill, so he drove me instead. At the top of the hill he told me to "Get your crap out of my car" and drove away. I went back a day later with a little gift to thank them.

The Ken-Mac house had no more than two students from any one country: two Americans, two Chinese, two Ghanaians and so on, though there were some Scottish and English students to balance things out. I had a Chinese roommate who called himself "George." He had left his wife and daughter in China to study for a PhD in architecture in Edinburgh.

When I asked him what his real name was, he told me "Fang."

Fang had never met a Jew in his life. This was a mind-blowing cultural experience for him. I wasn't just a Jew, but I was an out-wardly proud, Zionist Jew. I put up my pictures of Israel: of me in the army, my Israeli flag, my Hebrew-English dictionary, and a mezuzah on our door. I made myself at home.

My new friends all considered me Israeli, even though I was just an American who had spent a lot of time in Israel and went through most of Israeli army basic training.

I recall asking them which newspaper I should read. This was in 1991, when we still read old-fashioned newspapers. "Well, it depends," my British friends told me, "are you right or left wing?"

"Left, liberal, absolutely," I answered.

"In that case," they told me, "the *Guardian* is an excellent paper."

I bought the *Guardian* that morning. There was an article by Robert Fisk about an Israeli helicopter attack in Lebanon. It was graphic and made Israel look like a monster that just attacked poor Palestinians whenever they were bored.

The article made the picture on the front page look tame. I was aghast. I had never read such anti-Israel writing in my life. I went from South Florida, a bastion of Zionism and Jewish life, to New Jersey, an even larger bastion of Zionism and Jewish life, to Edinburgh, a city with one synagogue, no kosher food and a lot of people who hated Israel. I had never experienced anything like it.

It took me about a month before I understood the Scottish accent enough to understand what people were saying to me. Then I had the opposite problem: of getting people to understand me. I realized early on that I had to start adopting an English/Scottish accent or no one would understand me. I started by changing my vocabulary. Instead of saying "five-thirty" for 5:30, I said "half five." "Tomaytoes" became "tomaaatoes." I continued until I had developed a hybrid accent. It wasn't English or Scottish, but it certainly wasn't American anymore. I felt strange speaking this way, but everyone else thought it was normal.

My first day in the Arabic and Islamic Studies Department at the university was eventful, even though I never imagined it would be. The first thing I noticed, after going up the stairs to the department, was the sign on the front door. "We want to thank the government of Saudi Arabia for their generous funding." There were no signs like that at Rutgers. It was a literal sign of things to come.

I noticed that in every room in the department there was a map of the Middle East. Everything was accurate, except that the State of Israel had been replaced with a non-existent state called "Palestine." This was in 1990 and it wasn't a "politically correct" map, calling the "West Bank" and Gaza "Palestine," it was a map that simply wiped out the modern State of Israel.

One of my first questions to the Scottish professor after she finished the class was, "What happened to Israel on all of the maps in the department?" I doubted that she was so naïve as to not realize that it was deliberately replaced.

"Oh," she said, "I never paid attention before."

"Well," I asked her, "is it accurate? Let's check the date on the map. If it's from before 1948, I might understand."

It was from 1989. I asked the professor what she suggested. "I don't know. What do *you* think we should do?"

My answer was simple, "Get new maps; ones that have all of the countries in the modern Middle East on them." She agreed, and said she would speak to the head of the department about it.

I hadn't met the head of the department yet. Every time I went by his office to introduce myself he was either too busy to say "Hi" or he wasn't in.

After a few days, I asked the professor what was going on. She said she had submitted the request to the head of the department, but that there was no funding to purchase new maps for the whole department. They were very sorry, but the maps had to stay.

"Just use your imagination," she told me. "We all know that

Israel is there, it's just that the maps are off."

How could I solve this problem? Well, as the professor suggested, with a little imagination. I went to the library and photocopied the State of Israel from a map, cut out the edges, and pasted it onto all of the maps in the department. I did this early in the morning before anyone had showed up yet. The only disadvantage was that the maps were in color, but my photocopy was in black and white. That's what you get when there's no budget.

My first class of the day was with my Scottish professor. When all of the students came into the class and took their places, they looked at the map and saw what I had done.

An argument ensued. "It's not enough that you Jews stole Palestinian land, you also have to wipe Palestine off the map." I told them calmly that the State of Israel was an internationally recognized country but Palestine was not. "The maps were inaccurate. I just fixed them." It didn't end there. We agreed to wait until the professor came in and commented herself.

Class started without the professor noticing anything. When she went to write something on the chalkboard, she knew exactly what had happened. Turning to me, she said, "Barak, what is this?"

"You told me to use my imagination." She smiled and then continued teaching the class. When the class was over, we had a little conversation. She agreed to leave the map with my update.

As the day progressed, and I went from classroom to classroom, I noticed that all of the amendments I had made to the other maps had been removed. I wasn't too surprised; I kind of expected this. Thank God the photocopy machines were subsidized by the university. It cost almost nothing to make another twenty copies. I kept them in my backpack with some extra glue and tape.

The next time, I decided not to go early in the morning to literally "put Israel back on the map," but rather wait for a few minutes before class started. I went up to the front of the classroom and pasted my little black and white photocopy of Israel back on the map. Many times the professors would see me doing it. When I asked them, "Is there a State of Israel or not?" they had to admit there was.

The photocopies stuck around for a few more days. Then they were all gone again. When I got to my morning class my Scottish professor said, "You'll have to speak to the head of the department. He took them down himself."

His secretary asked me to wait, and then I was invited in. I was all smiles and very warm and friendly. He was colder than ice. The head of the department, it turns out, was an Arab-Palestinian-Muslim and he did not like this American-Israeli-Jew making a mess of his maps and his department.

I asked him the same question, "Is there a State of Israel or not?" He eventually agreed there was. "There's no need to worry," I said, "making photocopies is very cheap in the library. They're subsidized by the university." By the end of our short conversation, the photocopies went back up and would stay, at least until I left at the end of the school year.

One of my professors taught a course on the Modern Middle East. There was not a single discussion about Israel or Zionism or even Jews in the Arab world. When I asked the professor why he wasn't going to teach about Israel his answer was, "Israel is not part of the modern Middle East."

"Really?" I was shocked. "So what is it part of?"

He looked at me like I was from another planet, "Europe, of course. It's a European colony."

"A European colony, settled by which European country? France, Spain, Holland, England?" He changed the topic and didn't want to continue the conversation.

I went to the director of the overseas students department, who was responsible for the well-being of the American students from abroad. I asked her what she suggested I do. She was American, but had been living in Edinburgh for years. She wasn't Jewish or particularly a supporter of Israel, but she knew this wasn't okay.

"I've been waiting to place a complaint like this with the university administration for years," she said, rubbing her hands in glee. We placed a formal complaint about the maps and the course on the Modern Middle East. It was signed by both of us.

It took a couple of weeks and we got our answer. The professor would have to teach at least one class on the modern State of Israel. He was furious and tried to argue with the head of the department, who told him to either teach the class or find another job. The decision came down from the head of the administration and they had no choice.

A couple of months later, as it was getting closer to the end of the semester, the professor gave his class on Israel and Zionism. I figured the facts were the facts. I thought he'd talk about the Jewish roots to the ancient Land of Israel, the revival of the Hebrew language, the modern Zionist movement, and the wars Israel fought to defend itself from its Arab and Muslim neighbors. I almost expected him to let me teach the class.

Instead, it was a class about Israel's "war crimes against the Palestinians." He used the entire class to try to prove the Jews had no claim to the Land of Israel and that they were European colonists who stole the land from the poor, pitiful Palestinians.

The first time I tried to object or ask a question, he angrily shouted at me with a red face, "I've had enough of your troublemaking! You will not speak another word in my class." The other students didn't understand what was going on. They started sticking up for me.

"What did Barak do?" "All he did was ask a question." The pro-Palestinian students were actually defending my right to simply ask questions! It was a little mutiny. The professor didn't have a choice but to let me ask my questions. He answered them all with the same accusing manner as the rest of the class. The class ended, and that was the end of the topic of Israel in the Modern Middle East.

I had to do something. This was absurd, so I asked my first class professor what she suggested. "Give a talk on Zionism," she said. I had never thought of that. There were student-given talks all over campus in the evening hours. "Okay, how?" I asked. She told me that one of the accredited organizations on campus needed to sponsor me in order to speak on the university grounds.

I asked around and some friends who were a part of Amnesty International said they would sponsor me. "Former IDF Soldier Speaks about Zionism and Israel" was the title of the lecture that Amnesty International gave. The subtitle was, "Barak Hullman, a former soldier in the Israeli Army, will speak about the crimes committed by the State of Israel against the Palestinian people."

I strongly objected to the title since that wasn't what the talk was about at all, but the fliers had already been printed and were being hung around campus. I prepared for a few hours, making sure I got all of my historical dates and names right. I was going to give a brief overview of the Jewish connection to the Land of Israel and how all of these Jews ended up in the Middle East establishing their own state. Then I would talk about the different wars and conclude with the current peace talks in 1992.

I brought my own map of the modern Middle East and taped it up on the wall behind me. Some of my friends from the department said they would come. A few friends from the international house I lived in said they would come too. So, I figured there would be maybe fifteen or twenty people there.

When I arrived at the room, there was a crowd in the hallway. I had no idea what they were all doing there and gently worked my way into the room, only to discover it was packed from wall to wall with people and the crowd in the hallway was the overflow. There was space for probably a hundred people in the room, comfortably. But standing room only; there were at least 150 people there, and another fifty or so in the hallway.

The organizers from Amnesty International were visibly excited by the turnout. I was amazed and asked, "Who are all these people?" Many of them were clearly Muslim, others were Europeans with Palestinian shirts or scarves. It wasn't a crowd who had come to learn about Zionism, so it seemed like that subtitle worked. I didn't really know what to do. But my talk was prepared and I was going to give it over, regardless of the crowd.

I'm actually quite shy, but when I get in front of a crowd any shyness quickly disappears. I gave a great talk, and no one interrupted me. I was a regular at other lectures given by representatives and supporters of the Palestine Liberation Organization. I was constantly interrupting the speakers to ask questions about Israel and about statements they made. This crowd was much more polite than I was. I realized that these were Brits and I was an American-Israeli; very different cultures.

The organizers had made sure, before I gave the talk, that I would agree to take questions. Any politeness that I had been granted quickly flew out of the window. Every question was an attack. I was called names, told I had personally committed war crimes by serving in the IDF, and was interrupted during my responses. It wasn't pleasant, but I answered every question.

At one point one of the pro-Palestinian English students, who was wearing a "Palestine Will Be Free" t-shirt, asked me why I constantly pointed to the wrong country on the map when talking about Israel. I didn't understand the question. I pointed to Israel on the map and said, "This is Israel. What do you mean?" She said, "That's not Israel; Israel is over there to the right."

I asked her to come up front and show me Israel on the map. She had really lost her patience with me. She stormed up to the front and pointed to Saudi Arabia. "This is Israel, you fool," she told me in front of the crowd. There were some other students audibly supporting her. I asked her why she thought that country was Israel. "Because you stole so much land from the Palestinians!"

Saudi Arabia is one of the largest countries in the Middle East. Israel is a tiny sliver compared to it. I could understand her logic, but I asked her to read the name on the map for the country she was pointing to. "Saudi Arabia?" she said, with total shock.

Then I pointed to Israel and said, "This is Israel, where I've been pointing to all evening." She read the map and could not believe her eyes. Then she went to sit back down. I took more questions and could have kept going all night if they had allowed me, but the organizers said we had to vacate the room at a certain time and we were already an hour over. I left on a high I'd never experienced previously.

I had written for the newspaper at Rutgers, so I approached the university newspaper at Edinburgh and asked if I could write a column about Israel and Zionism. They agreed, but warned me that a lot of people would not be happy with what I planned on writing.

I had a biweekly column that became one of the most controversial columns in the student newspaper that year. I started to become very popular on campus. Not everyone hated Israel; some people even loved Israel, they were just afraid to say so. They'd never seen anything like me on campus before and they just wanted me to know that I had their silent support. Others simply admired my chutzpah. I loved the attention and had more girlfriends that year than in my whole life up until that point. Coming to Edinburgh, it turned out, was a very good decision.

One day, during the semester break, I ran into the director of the overseas department. "Wait until you get back to the department after the break," she said, so excited she could hardly hold back her enthusiasm. "What?" I asked. "Just wait, you'll see."

A short time later I was back for the new semester. All of my black and white photocopies were gone, but in their stead were brand new maps of the modern Middle East, with Israel in color. The university had sponsored the new maps against the objections of the head of the department.

It wasn't long before my next adventure in the department of Arabic and Islamic studies at the University of Edinburgh began. Arabic was a big deal in the department. I studied a lot of Arabic. Besides studying written classical Arabic, we had private sessions where we practiced speaking in it. There were two sweet, Sudanese Arabic teachers who we spent a lot of time with.

They didn't know that I was Jewish. Normally, I wore a kippah, but in Edinburgh, I was told to wear a hat so as not to make myself a target for anti-Jewish attacks. It was actually the Israeli rabbi of the Orthodox shul who asked me not to wear my kippah in public, though I didn't like it. At this point, my parents were getting very nervous about my safety, but I was twenty years old. Safety was the least of my concerns. Since I wore a hat in class over my kippah, these Sudanese Arabic teachers didn't know I was Jewish.

One day I saw one of them reading a book in Arabic. On the cover was an image of the State of Israel. A religious-looking Jew with big ears and a large nose was coming out of it and devouring Lebanon. There was blood dripping down the fangs of his mouth.

My Arabic wasn't good enough to understand what the book was about, so I asked the Sudanese Arabic teacher, in English, to please tell me what he was reading. "I'm reading about how the Zionists are taking over Lebanon." I wasn't dismayed at this anymore. He went on and on about how terrible "the Zionists" were and how they were the "cancer of the world." I told him that I'm a Jew and a Zionist. He didn't believe me. "You?" he said, shaking his head and smiling. "You're too nice to be a Zionist." We were very friendly up until that point. Then I took off my hat and showed him my kippah.

He immediately jumped up, kicking back his chair and shouted, "Jew! Get out of my classroom!" Now, I was absolutely shocked. I couldn't even believe this was happening to me. I'm writing this twenty-five years later and I *still* cannot believe this happened to me.

He pushed me out of the classroom, and then locked the door behind me. I could hear the other students demanding he let me back in, but the teacher would not budge. I went to the head of the department to complain. He came back to the classroom and asked that the teacher open the door. The two of them started arguing in Arabic. I didn't understand enough to know what they were saying but, since they were both pointing at me, I had an idea.

The head of the department actually apologized to me. He said, "We don't like Zionists here, but we have no problem with Jews. This is clearly not alright. I will have a chat with him, and this will be resolved by tomorrow." Many of the other students wanted to know what happened. They were as stunned as me.

The next day I showed up to class. This was a little classroom on the top floor of the building which was like a tall townhouse. There were about six floors in the building and the department took up three of them. This was the room in the roof with a little gable sticking out. There were maybe five students in the class, all waiting outside the door.

The teacher stood at the door. He said, "I will call the students and they will enter in the order that I call their names." He called them, "Robert, Suzie, Sarah and John." The four students came into the room, and then he locked the door. I knocked on the door and demanded to be let in. "No Zionists in my class!" he shouted from the other side.

I immediately went to the head of the department. He wasn't in. So I went to my early morning professor whose husband, it turned out, was the head of the administration that was receiving my complaints. She said she already knew about the situation because her husband had told her about my complaint. She would take care of it.

The next day, the second Arabic teacher was there. He was a sweet man and liked me as much as the first one (before he learned that I was a Jew and a Zionist). I told him right when I walked in the room, "I'm a proud Jew and a Zionist. If you have a problem with that, tell me right now." He smiled, shook my hand, and said, "I'm just here to teach Arabic, not to talk politics." We became good friends by the end of the year.

The first teacher was suspended, then eventually fired permanently. Since he was there from Sudan and now unemployed, he had to leave the country. The second teacher took over the full course load for the rest of the year.

Back at Rutgers, when I had asked to go to Edinburgh, the administrator had told me that studying abroad would give me a new perspective that I could never gain by just staying in the US. I didn't realize how right he was.

My year in Edinburgh was filled with such highs and lows. On the one hand I was becoming the adult I would be today, finding out what excited me in life, who I was and wanted to be. But on the other hand, I had some of the most boring, lonely moments of my life in Edinburgh.

Many times, the weekends would come and everyone would go home. The UK isn't a very big country and it has an excellent train system. Within a few hours, you could be just about anywhere in the country. I didn't have family in the UK but a couple of times, friends would take me home with them. The rest of the year I was on my own in the Ken-Mac house, with the African students who also had no place to go.

Of course, I had *Shabbos*. I wasn't entirely alone for the weekends. I spent *Shabbos* with the Jewish community in Edinburgh.

I knew the address, having looked at a map, and it was pretty straightforward where the shul should be. However, when I reached the address, 4 Salisbury Street, I found number 2 and number 6, but number 4 was missing. There was a very large-looking mansion with grounds between 2 and 6 but it didn't look like a synagogue.

After looking at every building surrounding where number 4 should be, I decided to go into the private property, walk through the courtyard, and knock on the large wooden door of the mansion.

No one answered, so I walked a little around the building, looking for another door or a window to peek into. I couldn't find one. All of the windows were covered on the ground level and no other doors looked inviting.

I came back and tried again. I knocked for a while, until someone came and opened a little window toward the top of the front door. It was a middle aged Scottish woman who didn't look Jewish at all. "What do you want?" she shouted at me.

"Um, sorry for bothering you ma'am."

She didn't have any patience for me. "I said: 'What do you want?' Go away from here!" and she closed the window in the door.

I knocked again and she reopened the window. "I'm looking for the synagogue. I've been walking around for half an hour now and I can't find it. Please, you have to help me. Did it move?" She looked at me for a minute and said, "What's your name? Where are you from?" I told her my name is Barak and I was an overseas student from the States studying there for the year. She looked at me again and said, "Wait here. Don't go anywhere." Then she closed the window.

In the meantime, it was already dark and the Jewish Sabbath had started. I had some food back at home, but I was really disappointed that I had missed the Friday night service for probably the first time in my life.

A few minutes later, someone else answered the door. It was an older man. He was Israeli and spoke to me in Hebrew. I was astounded. Having spent the last couple of years studying Hebrew and the summer in Israel, my Hebrew wasn't great, but it was good enough to have a conversation. I told him I was looking for the shul and asked what in the world was going on here? The older man told the Scottish woman to open the door.

There were a few other people standing behind the door and they looked relieved. I had no idea what was going on. They didn't say. They showed me into a little *beit midrash* (study room) where the Friday night service was in the middle. I was warmly welcomed. It was a small, tight-knit community where everyone knew each other. It was also an aging community so, when they saw me—young and full of potential—they were excited.

Several of the men had served in WWII. This sweet, grandfatherly man helped me find my way in the services. They used a different *siddur* from what I knew and I was totally lost. I noticed he was missing all of his fingers on his right hand. He also had scars on his arms. Eventually, someone told me it was from the War. He wasn't the only older man in the community who carried injuries from all those years ago.

Immediately after I walked into the *beit midrash*, people started arguing. I had to ask someone what they were arguing about—since half the conversation was in Yiddish and the other half in Scottish English, neither of which I understood. He told me, "You. We don't have a lot of guests around here. Everyone will want to host you eventually." By the end of that year, I had had Friday night dinners at almost every family in the community.

The rabbi was determined to get me more involved in the

synagogue during my year in Edinburgh. He was Israeli, indeed, as Israeli as they get. He had been a rabbi in Israel and, after retiring, took the position as the only rabbi in Edinburgh. The community provided him with a small apartment near the shul. At first I just came for Friday night services, but that was quickly rectified by the rabbi. Before I knew it, I was attending the Saturday morning services as well.

The first Saturday morning service was a real eye opener for me. The same building that I couldn't find at night was hiding a beautiful stained glass wall that could only be seen from the inside of the shul. It was a grand, old synagogue that had once been built for a large and thriving community, but those days were clearly over.

One of the most striking memories: there were two old top hats which sat on stands next to the doors of the ark, where the Torah scrolls are kept. The men that opened it had to wear the top hats before they opened the ark. I'd never seen anything like it. There was always a debate about whether to keep wearing the top hats, and whether someone who refused to wear one would still be allowed to take the Torah scroll out of the ark. There was often one person who would insist on wearing a top hat, whereas another insisted on *not* wearing one.

I figured by Sunday morning my time with the Jewish community was over until the next Friday night. But around eight o'clock Sunday morning, there was a knock at my door. I ignored it, of course. Then it came again, and again, until I finally opened the door. It was the rabbi. I was surprised. "Rabbi. What are you doing here?" He seemed relieved and exhausted at the same time.

"You have no idea how hard it was to find you," the rabbi said. "We need you for the *minyan*."

It turns out that the tenth man, who normally made the quorum of ten needed to say communal Jewish prayers, was sick and had ended up in the hospital. Someone had to say *kaddish*. They needed a tenth man and it was me.

The first night when I went to shul, I told the rabbi where I was living, but never expected him to visit me early Sunday morning. Before I realized it, I was at the Sunday morning *minyan* every week, even when they didn't need me. "Just in case," I was told.

I was also there Thursday nights, working in the communal kitchen. Since there was no kosher food in Edinburgh, the community would bake challahs for anyone who wanted. We would bake twenty or thirty at a time. The students would do the baking and the shul became my second home.

Unfortunately, during that year (as in previous years and years since), the shul was firebombed with Molotov cocktails. It was also vandalized with anti-Israel graffiti on a regular basis. Having grown up in South Florida, I'd never before experienced anti-Jew hatred like that before and it still shocks me to this day. After the first firebombing, I understood why the community was so cautious in hiding the shul from the outside and not letting just anyone in.

There were times when our *davening* was interrupted by Molotov cocktails and other times by protests outside of the shul. I joined the community as we prepared to defend ourselves from a small crowd of anti-Israel protesters that were trying to break down the door.

It wasn't an easy place to be a Jew, especially a proud one. I decided to wear my kippah without a hat on the walk to shul as a sign of rebellion against the anti-Semitism. The Jewish Sabbath starts with the sunset. In the winter, Shabbat started at 3 pm and I would have to leave my Arabic class to get to shul on time.

My Scottish Arabic teacher lived near the shul. Oftentimes, I would see her coming home from the class I'd left early as I was walking to a family's house for the Friday night meal. She always told me it was dangerous to walk around the streets like that with a kippah on and that I should really reconsider. But she must have known that I was young and foolish and would never have agreed. Now, at forty-four, I'm not sure if I would have changed a thing.

Meanwhile, back at the International House, Fang and I were slowly getting to know each other. In order for Fang to get his PhD in Edinburgh, he had to leave his wife and daughter behind in China as collateral. His English was horrible. I have no idea how he got into a doctoral program in the UK with such poor English.

His dissertation was going to be on British influences on Chinese architecture. He was writing his dissertation by copying entire paragraphs from other people's works. He would literally take an entire page, or several pages from someone else's book and copy it into his dissertation. Then he would ask me to check it and make sure he did a good job with his English.

Eventually, I realized what he was doing and told him it was plagiarism. He had no idea what I was talking about. That's how he got into the PhD program; why would it be a problem to keep doing it? I spent many nights rewriting Fang's dissertation. He couldn't find enough ways to thank me.

Fang made a little feast for himself every night, but never invited anyone to eat with him. We all ate our student food while we watched him slowly enjoy a Chinese feast that most restaurants couldn't copy. Once I gave him a compliment on how good his food looked, and he realized that this was a way to thank me for helping him with his dissertation.

The next night, he made double the feast and invited me to join him. All of my friends in the house were jealous. He had really made an effort, with lots of beef and very special dumplings and a soup. However, I am a vegetarian. I wouldn't eat anything he made. He apologized profusely. "Tomorrow night I make new meal without meat," he said, with a big smile. In the meantime, my friends in the house happily helped Fang finish the meal.

The next night he made another feast, this time with chicken. After the huge effort I had to tell him, again, I couldn't eat it because I don't eat chicken. He was totally confused. It told him I don't eat beef or chicken or fish. "No problem," he said, not allowing me to defeat him, "tomorrow night, new meal; no beef, no chicken, no fish."

The next night, he did it all over again, making a huge feast. He wanted it to be a surprise, so I wasn't allowed in the kitchen until he was done. This time he had made everything with shrimp and crabs. What was I going to say? I had to tell him, yet again, that I don't eat any animals.

"But there's no beef, no chicken, no fish." He was smiling, so I knew he wasn't offended. Besides, my friends were waiting at the entrance of the kitchen ready to finish off the meal they knew I wasn't going to eat.

The next night, he got it right and we had a delicious vegetarian Chinese feast. The one nice thing that came out of all of these miscommunications was that Fang realized everyone loved his cooking. Before long he was having more and more of the students in the house over for his meals. Everyone appreciated him even though we could hardly understand a word of what he said.

Eventually, Fang and I became very good friends. I learned a little Chinese, which made him incredibly happy, and he learned a lot about Jews and Israel. He had never met a Jew in his life before.

When winter came, I got a stomach virus like I had never experienced in my life. My Scottish friends said I had to have an old Scottish remedy that solved every health problem: whisky with hot water, honey and some other stuff they threw in there. I forget what they called it, but it had some Gaelic name. I drank it down and went to sleep. The next morning, the doctor had to be called because I was in such bad shape I could hardly move. He checked me out and said there was clearly something going on in my stomach, but that it would probably pass on its own and I should just rest in bed until then.

The doctor left and I felt like I was going to die. Fang, being my roommate, saw all of this and decided to take matters into his own hands. He had a huge selection of Chinese medicine pills that he had brought with him: several tackle boxes of pills. Each had a different color and many had pictures of animals and other symbols on them. He looked in one of his Chinese medicine books and came up with the concoction he thought would heal me. He gave me about twenty pills and said to drink them down. I thought this might kill me, so I called my friends in and asked them to witness as I took the pills so they'd know who killed me.

Several of the pills had deer on them. I asked my friends if they thought I should take them. "No way," they all said, "you have no idea what's in there." With that, I swallowed them all down and went to sleep. I slept better than I had in a long time and woke up entirely cured. My friends and I were all in shock. Fang was very pleased with himself. His English writer and friend was back. It was as if someone had pressed a reset button. Not only did I feel better, I felt better than I had in a long time. I also didn't get sick the whole rest of the year I was in Edinburgh.

Fang always invited me to do Tai Chi with him in the garden outside of the house, but I never did. I would watch him from the window though, along with several of my fellow students.

There was this one guy from Ghana, whose name was "Blackie." His name was really Seth, but he wanted to be called "Blackie." We told him it was racist, but he insisted. He was so impressed with my curly hair, since he'd never met a white, non-African with curly hair as tight as mine—he stored pens and other handy items in his own. When he saw that I could also store pens in my hair, we became good friends.

It was Blackie that became Fang's Tai Chi partner, but only in fair weather. Fang, however, did his Tai Chi even when it was raining or snowing. I'll never forget the whole house standing by the windows, watching Fang doing Tai Chi in piles of snow, with the snow coming down on him.

When I got to Edinburgh, one of the first groups I joined was the Jewish Society. There were maybe fifteen of us and not everyone was Jewish. One woman (who later became one of my serious girlfriends that year) was there because her boyfriend, who was studying abroad in Japan, was Jewish. Just like me, to date one of the few non-Jews in the Jewish Society. We had the full spectrum of religious and political beliefs amongst the Jews in our tiny group. We got along as friends, but we never agreed on anything politically. I considered myself left wing back then, but I was really a centrist without realizing it.

It didn't really matter what my political views were. In the first meeting, they had elections for the Society's officers and I was elected the spokesperson without even being asked. "What? Why me?" I asked after it was announced that I was unanimously elected, without ever running. The answer was clear and obvious, "Because you're American and have a big mouth." That was a nice welcome. I decided that even though I wasn't *that* American, and wasn't *that* loud-mouthed, I would take on the challenge. I had no idea what was in store.

That year, the university administration decided to ban any society that was deemed racist. The United Nations passed a resolution in 1975 saying that "Zionism is a form of racism." It was revoked by the United Nations in 1991. This was 1990, so the resolution was still active.

The decision by the university was a problem for us since we were proudly Zionist and pro-Israel. It didn't take long for the university to send us a notice that, unless we could prove otherwise, we were considered a racist organization and would be banned on campus. We chose to try to prove otherwise and, after a long process of about six months, it was going to be brought to a student vote before approximately 3,000 students at the university.

As the official spokesperson for the Jewish Society that year, I went to every Israel/Palestine related event and shared some pro-Israel point of view. However, with the university deciding to bring our objection to a debate in front of the entire student body, my role as spokesperson was taken to a whole new level.

The way the system at the university worked was that one of the other societies had to claim that your society was racist, and then ask the university to ban you. It's almost hard for me to believe, but we were being banned by the Socialist Workers Party.

I was confused and asked other students why the socialists would hate us. Most of us were also socialists; I was at the time. The answer was simple and astonishing. The Socialist Workers Party is a euphemism for the Nazi party. The student society of the Nazis was demanding that the Jewish Society—because of our support for Zionism and the State of Israel—be banned for racism.

It was absurd and ironic, but we had to face the reality that two other Jewish societies had already been banned on two other Scottish university campuses. The planned debate was to be between two students, one from the Socialist Workers Party and one from the Jewish Society, which, of course, meant me.

I prepared for the debate by reading as many history books about the conflict as I could find. However, as convinced as I was about the facts, finding a message that would resonate with a large group of anti-Israel students was getting harder and harder. I couldn't figure it out. What was I going to say that would prove that Zionism wasn't racism? What would convince these 3,000 students? I was getting stressed. I asked my student friends in the Jewish Society for help but they just patted me on the back, "Good luck, man, you're going to need it."

Then it hit me. How did I become a Zionist? By reading the book *Exodus* by Leon Uris. It's the greatest piece of Jewish propaganda ever produced. Fang, who knew what I was preparing for, was constantly upset at me for using a novel to prepare for my debate. "But everything I want to say was already said here." I told him, exasperated. "Why should I try to reinvent it myself?"

I read the book over and over again like it was the Bible. I took notes; I memorized lines word by word. I had the book with me on my chair as I was waiting to be called up to the stage for the debate, going over my notes. I ignored Fang's objections and continued, focused on the goal of winning a debate that was nearly unwinnable.

A few days before the debate, we learned that the Socialist Workers Party would not be represented by a student, but rather a lawyer from London who was hired specifically to make an example of the Jewish Society at Edinburgh. The other two campuses where the Jewish Society had been banned were not considered big league, serious universities, but Edinburgh was. It was the number three university in the UK, after Oxford and Cambridge. To ban the Jewish Society at Edinburgh would be a huge accomplishment for the Socialist Workers Party and make it much easier for them to ban other Jewish Societies across the UK.

How could we debate against a lawyer from London? The fact that the lawyer was coming from London made it even more impressive in their eyes. We looked into hiring our own lawyer, but none of them seemed like they were going to do a very good job. They didn't know the facts well enough and weren't really on our side; just a gun for hire.

The night of the debate came. The student hall was packed from wall to wall, with students sitting on the stairs, standing in the hallways and even outside. Instead of being scared, I was exhilarated. This has happened to me as long as I can remember. I become a different person when I stand in front of a crowd. The bigger the crowd, the more exciting it is for me. This was the biggest crowd I'd ever spoken in front of, and I was flying.

I walked into the hall and it was like a boxing match. Everyone made way for me to get to the stage and looked at me like they were ready to eat me alive. They'd already made up their minds before

I walked in. They were just there to watch me be slaughtered by the lawyer from London before they placed their vote in favor of us being racists and then finished drinking their pints of beer. I didn't expect that almost everyone would have a glass of beer in their hands. Beer was being served on draft in the Student's Hall. The bartenders could hardly keep up with the demand. After being six months in Scotland, I shouldn't have been surprised, but I was.

I was first on the stage and waited for the lawyer from London to appear, expecting a dapper man in a three-piece suit with a watch on a chain. Instead, it was a young woman wearing a simple red dress and short heels. She didn't seem so intimidating to me, but she wasn't happy. She never smiled. The more I looked at her, the more I realized that she was all business and here to win.

The debate began by introducing us. The lawyer from London was introduced as the representative from the Socialist Workers Party; the students were not impressed. This was meant to be a debate between students, not a debate between a lawyer and a student. Some students verbally objected but were told that it was allowed within the university's rules. They were told that the Jewish Society was also allowed to bring a lawyer to debate their side, but chose to be represented by a student instead.

The lawyer from London got up and made her arguments. When she finished, she received a polite round of applause. Then I was introduced as a student from overseas studying in the university, who had served in the Israeli army, was studying Arabic and Islam, and had a column in the student newspaper. Only my friends from the Jewish Society applauded as I came forward to speak. The rest of the room of 3,000 students were either too busy talking with each other or staring at me, ready to watch me make a fool of myself.

I've thought about this moment many times since, and I really don't remember what I said. It must have been the weeks of preparation and the adrenaline. As I sat down, I knew I couldn't have done any better. We were allowed to answer questions from the crowd and I answered them like I did in the talks I gave earlier in the year: simply and honestly. The debate ended, and now the students had to vote. The vote was tallied within a short time.

I knew we had no chance of winning. Now that my job was over, I was relieved and already thinking of the little party we'd have in a local pub after the results were announced. Those of us in the Jewish Society would still be Jews and Zionists. We could meet off campus. We would still be friends. We just wouldn't have our Jewish Society.

The results were announced. "Regarding the resolution before this house that the Jewish Society is racist because of its support for Zionism, this house votes that the Jewish Society is *not* racist and may remain on campus." Holy cow. We won! I won. I was in shock. I didn't understand what had just happened. The lawyer from London stormed off the stage and said she would be appealing the decision. The students went back to their drinking—pleased with their handiwork—and I became a hero on campus.

For the rest of the year I never paid for another drink. Every time I went out to a pub someone wanted to buy me a drink and talk about the debate. I also had a string of beautiful girlfriends after that. It was literally one of the greatest moments of my life.

Just for that, it was worth the whole year in Edinburgh. Amazingly, the other Jewish Societies were able to use our win to prove they also were not racist, and were reinstated on the two campuses where they had been banned. I met the lawyer from

London in the pub where we were celebrating after the debate. She came over to me to congratulate me on winning the debate.

"How did you pull that off?" she said, smiling for the first time. "Honestly, I have no idea," and that was the truth. I can guess now, in retrospect. I probably did make valid points, but it was really the students that wanted to send a message to the university: if you want to have a debate between students, let it stay between students.

I went out with my friends from the Jewish Society on one of my last nights in Edinburgh. It was sad for us to part. We had become very close friends that year. One of them suggested that we didn't need to be sad because all of us were going to meet in Jerusalem after we graduated. I had one more year at Rutgers. They had one more year in Edinburgh, but we had each other's emails. With that we hugged and parted.

My first few years in Jerusalem, I looked for my friends. The emails we had at university were cancelled when we graduated, so I asked my friends from the UK in Jerusalem if they knew my friends from Edinburgh. At least for the first few years, I was the only one that actually moved to Israel.

I'm glad I took my father's advice. This was the stepping stone that took me some place I never would have gone otherwise.

PLAY A CHASSIDIC MELODY
BEFORE EACH CLASS

A quality life is a balancing act. You need responsibility, but also freedom. How can you have a house, family, job and community, and still have the freedom to feel that you're not a slave to your life? It's a balancing act, just like the high wire.

Some people get so bogged down with the responsibilities of their lives that they eventually break. They leave their kids and run off with someone else or to find something else. I came to the realization years ago that I need to make my current life the one I want to live, or else why am I even living it?

I want to live where I want, not where I should or where it is reasonable. As a result we live in a small house. There are nine of us living in a house that would probably be comfortable for two or three—with one bathroom.

This can be a challenge at times. There are sometimes "accidents" next to the bathroom door, or sometimes my kids use the public garden outside. You know, fertilizer. Five girls sleep together in what used to be my office. The two boys sleep in what used to be the other half of our bedroom. But the kids are happy, and I would be miserable any place else.

My wife has made the best of my decision to stay in our small house in the center of town. I once asked my parents when I was young why we lived in the house I grew up in, in the suburbs of North Miami Beach, instead of someplace exciting like Coconut

Grove or South Beach? My father told me they wanted to live in Coconut Grove (a hippie haven full of eccentric people), but they chose to live where I grew up because it was "more reasonable." I was always so disappointed that we didn't live someplace more exciting. So, when I became an adult, I chose to live where I really wanted, despite the space disadvantage.

For years, I worked a job I hated. I didn't have a choice. My wife stays at home, we have seven kids and both a house and debts to pay off. I couldn't afford to leave my job. I did the best I could, slowly making sure I worked more and more on my own without any supervision. This went on for years, until the job ended. I lost my income, but I gained the freedom to pick a new path of making a living.

The temptation of taking a new, miserable job was enormous. I even applied for a few and sent my resume off to headhunters. There were many companies that wanted to hire me, but, of course, they weren't in Jerusalem. Just the thought of four hours of commuting to Tel Aviv, or further, convinced me to stop applying for jobs. Also, I was so burned out after working a job I hated for so many years. I couldn't devote a full day of work to something I didn't love, even if I wanted to. I'd probably end up in an early grave.

I suffered for years with a lack of sufficient income, but I was determined to make it with my business. After three years of struggling, I figured it out. I've been making a living doing what I enjoy for about a year now. It's not always a pleasure, but I work much less than I used to and make a lot more, probably three times as much. Most of the time, I really enjoy my work. I chose it after a lot of thought and contemplation.

I am willing to take risks and embarrass myself, even though I'm pretty shy at heart. These little risks make life a thrill. For example, my leading the *davening* in shul. I didn't grow up in a religious home, so leading the *davening* in a proper Orthodox shul was very intimidating. The first year was so hard; I don't know why anyone let me keep leading the *davening*. But they did, and now I'm the regular leader in two shuls.

I also decided to learn to play the guitar at thirty-five. Then, after a few lessons, I brought my guitar to a Torah lesson and volunteered myself to play a Chassidic melody before each class. For years I was so nervous; it could be snowing outside, but I would be dripping sweat. My fingers could not find the right chords. There was always someone in the lesson who was a great guitar player and you could see the pain on their faces when I would play.

But I made a rule for myself: once I start something that I want to do or be, I just keep going. I tell people I'm like the Energizer bunny. I just keep going. I hit a wall, I turn around and keep going until I hit the next wall. I just don't stop. By doing this, I've made my life exciting, without sacrificing my family or responsibilities.

Right now, I'm sitting in a restaurant writing this book. I realized that the only way I could write this book is if I forced myself to stay away from home and work and anything else that might distract me. So, the day before, I arrange everything at work to take time off and go to a restaurant or hotel lobby to write. If I didn't, I'd never write.

I'm busy. Everyone is busy. You can go through your whole life and never get around to what you really want to do. You can live your whole life "responsibly," and never be the person you always wanted to be.

If you're not living the life you want right now, what are you living for? You don't have to drop everything and run away. That's not a balanced life. But you do need to make sure you're doing some of the things you want, right now, every day, or at least every week. Make sure you're living a life of meaning. If there's something you don't like, make a change. Make little changes, until you eventually get to where you want to be. Then, just like climbing any mountain, you'll see the next peak; the next goal you want to reach once you've passed this summit.

SLAY THE GREEK GODS

As the year I spent in Edinburgh was coming to an end, there were posters on campus announcing a summer camp fair where American summer camps were recruiting staff from the UK to come and work for the summer. I had been working at summer camps for years. Maybe I could get a job at the fair, even though I'm not from the UK.

I didn't mind working at a non-Jewish camp but, when I saw there was a Jewish camp recruiting, I headed straight toward their table. The camp director was there. He was a tall, middle-aged man. He didn't look religious at all. At that point I always had my head covered either with a kippah or a hat. I told him that I was a student for the year in Edinburgh, but I was heading back to the States in a month and was looking for a camp to work at for the summer.

I told him I was a passionate Zionist, had defended Israel on campus all year, and had a column in the university newspaper. I was also an Eagle Scout, which made a very strong impression on him. He told me that the camp kept kosher, kept *Shabbos* and would love to have someone like me on staff. My friends couldn't believe I was hired on the spot.

I went back to Miami after the year in Edinburgh, and then headed to upstate New York to the B'nai Brith summer camp. These summer camps were always literally in the middle of nowhere. Look for "nowhere" on the map, and you'll find it full of summer camps. Of course, in America there are always people living somewhere, but they were the furthest thing from city-raised American Jews.

Every time we stepped into a bar from camp, the culture shock was so abrupt it was like being woken up at 3 am when you thought you could sleep until 10.

It was even more abrupt for me that year, since I had just been totally immersed in the UK. I had taken on a hybrid American-English-Scottish accent, dress, and vocabulary. I wasn't American and I wasn't British. I was something in-between. Whenever someone would ask me if I realized this, I would say, "Do you reckon?" ending the sentence pitching up, just like I learned in Scotland. I wore Doc Martin shoes, shirts and pants I had bought in Edinburgh. While in Edinburgh, I blended in as an American who didn't stick out too much. In the States, I stood out like a Brit who fit into America. This is how I entered the Jewish summer camp in the New York boondocks.

I came to camp a couple of weeks early to help dust off the winter and turn the camp from a large attic into a summer camp. I got to know some of the staff. There were two programs; one was a more religious program for older kids and the other a more generally Jewish program for everyone. I was working in the general program. The religious program had daily prayer services and they invited me to join them. I had a pair of *tefillin* from my great grandfather and I had always wanted to use them.

I brought them to the summer camp hoping to put them to good use. This was my first time taking them out of the bag and probably the first time they had been used in fifty years. They weren't in such good shape. I didn't have enough of a Jewish education to know that they weren't even kosher anymore. They were a family heirloom, but no longer *tefillin*. Not knowing that, I took the old, dry leather boxes and straps and tried to put them on like everyone else was doing in the *minyan*. The leather straps disintegrated on my arms and head as I tried to put them on. I was so embarrassed.

Someone told me that this pair of *tefillin* wasn't kosher anymore, but I didn't want to believe it. They offered me a kosher pair to use. I couldn't part with my great grandfather's treasure and ended up leaving the service early. My pride kept me away for several weeks, until I decided that I was going to *daven* with the *minyan* every day and use their *tefillin*. It started me on a lifetime of *davening* with a *minyan* until today.

The kids finally arrived, and the summer began. I had never been to a somewhat religious Jewish summer camp; the Jewish summer camp I had attended as a kid was connected to the Reform movement. It had some type of religious services, but the Reform movement pretty much does whatever they like. This camp followed the basic rules of the Jewish religion, so it was very different.

I had been told that the camp kept kosher, kept *Shabbos* and other Jewish traditions. This was somewhat true, but not quite like the camp director had told me in Edinburgh. The food was kosher; I spent a lot of time in the kitchen because the camp director asked me to see that everything was. I was kind of like an external, unofficial *mashgiach* (kashrut supervisor) for the kitchen, even though I hardly knew anything about keeping kosher. It was more an education for me than it was me supervising anyone else.

Shabbos, however, wasn't what I had expected. There was special food made for *Shabbos* and everyone dressed in white. We had services on Friday night, but there was a debate the first time over whether to use a microphone or not. According to traditional Judaism, it is forbidden to use a microphone on the Sabbath but, according to the Reform movement, you can do anything you want. Since the camp was officially and historically traditional, using a microphone on *Shabbos* was not allowed. However, almost all of the staff and campers were not traditional, and they hated that we didn't use a microphone.

The service started out without a microphone and ended with one. Some of the staff and kids stormed out in protest, and the rest applauded and cheered that the camp was finally entering the 20th century. Even though I had grown up in the Reform movement, in university I had moved to the other side; the traditional side; the side of my great grandfather. I was not happy about the microphone, but I didn't storm out in protest. I stayed with my campers until the service was over. We went to the dining hall and had a somewhat traditional *Shabbos* meal.

Shabbos morning everyone was allowed to sleep in. I woke up early to join the religious group in their service and came back to the cabin before the kids and assistant staff had even opened their eyes.

The camp director's son had passed away a few weeks before the summer started. I didn't know the cause, but the effects on the director were apparent. He was a shell of the person I had met in Edinburgh. It was like he was replaced by a wax figure and I didn't know him well at all. People who knew him told me it was like he had a personality transplant. He had no energy, although he had a job that required the energy of three people.

I went to ask him about the microphone on *Shabbos* and, although he opposed it, he didn't have the strength to do anything about it. The camp that was meant to be somewhat religious quickly fell apart. *Shabbos* was hardly kept. The liberal forces at camp got their way in every area except for *kashrut* (keeping ko-sher), which was run by a group of religious men that wouldn't budge on their standards.

At first I just held my tongue, but as the camp's religious stan-dards got lower and lower, I couldn't stay quiet anymore. I reached my tipping point when the 9th of Av arrived.

The 9th of Av is the day in Jewish history when Jews fast and remember the destruction of the Holy Temple in Jerusalem in the year 70 CE. Many other Jewish tragedies also "coincidently" happened on that day. It was announced that the camp would be fasting, there would be no music played and many of the regular camp activities would be cancelled for the day.

The liberal staff members didn't like this at all. They raided the kitchen and served a meal to whoever wanted to eat, insisting that there was nothing to mourn since no one cared about the Temple in Jerusalem anymore anyway. The camp director tried to put his foot down. He said "Enough is enough," but the rebellious staff did whatever they liked and he didn't have the strength to stop them.

A few days later, we had a week of "color war." Traditionally in Jewish camps this is called the "Maccabiah," kind of like a Jewish Olympics. The camp is divided up into colors or tribes and every-one competes with each other for the week. I always hated these color wars, because they divided up the camp and the individual cabins. I had worked so hard on helping the kids in my cabin be-come a cohesive team. We had learned to love one another, but this color war would split us up.

I made it clear that the color war was only outside of the cabin. Inside we were all one family. I didn't want to hear a word about the color war once any of my campers stepped foot into the cabin. It worked fine for the first few days. Then my campers started getting tired of the color war. They wanted to do something together, as a cabin, like we'd been doing all summer. I was also tired of the color war. Just then, an opportunity presented itself like a bow-wrapped box delivered to the front door.

There were judges during the color war. Often they would dress up as some ancient figure. The same liberal forces that had been at work all summer decided that this summer would be the first time that the color wars would be judged by the "Greek gods." Since the Jews suffered enormously by the Greeks, and we don't believe in idol worship, we usually avoid Greek gods and their mythology. All five judges dressed up as Greeks in togas and wreaths and insisted that everyone bow down before them and kiss their hands. It wasn't serious, of course, and some of the other staff members went along with it, insisting that their campers comply.

I honestly could not believe that I was seeing this in a Jewish camp. The whole story of Chanukah is about the Jews rebelling and then defeating the Greek army who told them to bow down to their Greek gods and kiss their hands. Jews don't bow down to anyone except God. All through Jewish history, from Biblical to modern times, there are stories of Jews who refused to bow down to kings and other rulers.

In ancient Egypt, it is said in Jewish sources that the entrance to the Pharaoh's court was through a low passageway so that everyone who entered would have to bow down before Pharaoh, but when Avraham avinu (Abraham, our father) went to meet Pharaoh, the passageway raised up miraculously so Avraham could enter without out bowing down.

Many years later, Yaakov Avinu (Jacob, our father) came to

Egypt to meet another Pharaoh. The same thing happened. The passageway miraculously rose up so Yaakov could pass through without bowing. That's why, in the Bible, Pharaoh asks Yaakov, "How old are you?" somewhat in shock. There was a record of when this miracle had happened before to Avraham and, when his grandson, Yaakov, came, Pharaoh thought maybe it was the same person.

In the story of Purim, Mordechai refused to bow down to the king. There is story after story about Jews refusing to bow down. And here, at this little Jewish summer camp in upstate New York, Jews are bowing down to "Greek gods?" I could not believe it.

We had a staff meeting every night and I brought it up. Some of the staff supported me. Most of the staff thought I was a fanatic and told me to relax. I told them I could take a lot, but this was going way too far. I wouldn't stand for it. All five of the judges (the "Greek gods") were at the meeting. None of them thought it was a problem. They said to me, "Suck it up. That's how it is. The color war is over in two days anyway."

I came back to the cabin that night determined to change things, somehow. I told the kids in my cabin everyone was staying and not going to the color war as a protest against bowing down to the Greek gods. Then I told them the story of Chanukah and how the Maccabees defeated the Greek army and afterwards reestablished the services in the Temple and Jewish autonomy in the Land of Israel.

We took our sheets and dressed in togas like the judges. I brought a role of aluminum foil from the kitchen, and went to the crafts area to get paint, cardboard and scissors. I told the boys to make the most awesome cardboard swords and weapons they could. At the lunchtime meal, we were going to slay the Greek gods.

They *loved* this idea. They were more excited about my crazy plan to stop the bowing and kissing hands madness than anything they'd done all summer. Within an hour we were ready to go and practiced marching in unison outside of the dining hall. I had the kids singing Hebrew songs about the Jewish people never giving up.

We then marched into the dining hall and everyone stopped what they were doing. They thought it was part of the color war. We marched over to the judges dressed as Greek gods. I took one of their microphones and announced that our cabin had had enough of this hypocrisy.

"Jews don't bow down to anyone, especially to Greek gods." Then I told the boys, "Draw your weapons" and everyone pulled out the cardboard and aluminum weapons they had made an hour earlier. I cried out, "Boys, slay the Greek gods. Show no mercy!" and my sweet thirteen-year-old boys had the time of their lives attacking the judges.

Everyone applauded us. The boys in my cabin became the most popular kids in camp. Many of them proudly told me they got their first kisses after that. Every kid in the cabin that wanted a girlfriend had one. The cabin itself was united like no other group of kids in camp, and then a few days later I was fired.

I was moved to the maintenance crew; kept away from the kids. The kids that were in my cabin for the first session of camp always sought me out, but the kids in the second session had no idea who I was. That's how the summer ended. After that, I went back to Rutgers College to finish my last year of my B.A.

As soon as I reached the campus, however, I realized that there were more Greek gods to slay. Within a short amount of time I got my inspiration back.

THE COIN FROM
SHABBOS MINCHA

I have a regular seat in the shul where I *daven* for *mincha* (the afternoon prayer) on *Shabbos* afternoon. It's right next to the *shtender*. The shul was built around seventy years ago. They're still proud of the fact that it was the first shul in the neighborhood to have an air conditioner. In addition to the air conditioner, they also put in wood panels, halfway up the wall. That was pretty fancy forty years ago.

The *shtender*, where the *chazzan* (prayer leader) *davens*, is pretty small. It has two candle holders that seem like they were made to have electric lights on top of them. I don't think they ever actually held candles. They sit on a piece of wood that holds them in place. From my place, when I stand up, I can see what's under the piece of wood holding the electric candlesticks.

There are plenty of dead bugs. Maybe they're seventy-year-old bugs? There are some screws, lots of dust, and that's about it. For years I've been peering into that space under the wood that holds the electric candle holders without noticing anything special. Then one day, to my utter surprise, I saw an old Israeli lira coin. These coins have been out of circulation for probably fifty years. They're not worth very much. You can buy them from coin collectors for probably twenty dollars or so. Still, it was incredibly exciting to see this coin in a place where no one had seen it for so long.

My first instinct was to take the coin. But it was *Shabbos*, so

I'd have to wait until *Shabbos* was over. While I was waiting for *Shabbos* to end, I kept thinking about how that coin ended up there. Was it placed there intentionally? Maybe someone found it and wanted to donate it to the shul, however, the *Tzedakah* box was outside of the shul. There was no reason to leave it there under the wood.

Then I thought it must have been someone who showed up to shul just before *Shabbos*, and realized he had a coin in his pocket. Since it's forbidden to carry or use money on *Shabbos*, he probably said to himself that he'll just put it here under the wood of the electric candle holders and pick it up after *Shabbos*. Of course, his *Shabbos* was so high, by the time *motzei Shabbos* (the end of *Shabbos*) came, he totally forgot about that coin. Maybe he never *daven*ed in this shul again? Maybe it was his last *Shabbos* on this earth? Who knows, but the coin is still there, all these years later.

How many other people have seen this coin before me? I couldn't have been the only one. Other people sat in that same place before I was even born. Someone must have changed the light bulbs on the candle holders, or had to fix the electricity or something before my discovery. Why did they leave the coin there?

Maybe they had the same thought as me. If I took it, no one else would have the thrill of discovering it. The thrill was not that I could own this coin, but that everyone else before me had left it there for me to discover. So, come *motzei Shabbos*, instead of taking the coin, I moved the wood holding the candle holders a little, just enough to cover the coin, so that sometime in the future, someone else could have the thrill of discovering it, just like I did.

YOU ONLY MAKE
ONE SOUND

When I was in 12th grade my favorite class was English. I had an amazing teacher who was much more than a teacher; she was a mentor. She took a personal interest in her students and encouraged us to grow. She was creative, and most of the classes were interesting. I was into creative writing at the time. Often, she would read my poems and other pieces to all of her classes, including the advanced placement (college level) class, which gave me a great deal of pride since I was such a horrible student. It was only because of classes like this that I even passed high school.

One day this teacher asked us to do a skit for the class. The class was divided up into groups, and we planned our skits. In my skit there needed to be several people speaking foreign languages. One person spoke Spanish, another French, and I was supposed to speak Hebrew. I didn't speak Hebrew back then, so I just said some Hebrew words that I had learned in synagogue. We performed our skit, and then it was another group's turn.

One of the kids in the group talked about the shofar. A shofar is a musical instrument made out of a ram's horn. It is used mainly on Rosh Hashanah and it is difficult to play. The shofar has a very small mouthpiece. It's nearly impossible to get a sound out of it unless you've practiced a lot.

The student, a friend of mine from school and synagogue, asked the class to give it a try. He demonstrated himself that it was possible to make a sound, although it wasn't so great. He dared anyone to try to get a sound out of the shofar. Many students got up and tried. They blew air into the shofar, made their faces red, but no sound came out. If it did, it either sounded like a dying cow or high-pitched whisper.

I had spent my entire school career as a shy kid who got along with everyone but was never very popular. Finally, there was something that I excelled at: blowing the shofar. So, I asked for a chance. This kid gave me the shofar and I blew it like a pro. There's an entire order of playing the shofar (even though you only make one sound with it) and I played the whole thing, loudly and clearly.

I expected all of the kids in the class to give me a standing ovation. I finished and there was silence. I looked at the class and they looked angrily at me. "Barak!" they practically shouted, "what's wrong with you?" What? I thought to myself. What did I do wrong? Then I looked over at my friend and saw that his face was red. I had embarrassed him.

He was supposed to be the expert at blowing the shofar, and he thought no one else would be better than him. Everyone in the class also knew this, but I didn't realize it until then. I apologized right away, but it was too late. My friend was embarrassed and there was no going back. He accepted my apology and even asked me to show him how I blew the shofar so well, but the other kids were angry at me.

What was the purpose of me blowing the shofar? To show that I could do it? I didn't need to prove that to myself. I also didn't need to prove it to the kids in class. I just wanted to show off. That would have been fine, if it didn't embarrass the kid whose presentation I had just messed up.

It happens sometimes that I'm embarrassed by other people, and I think back to this memory. I try to be forgiving and understanding. I also realize that every time someone embarrasses me, it's a reminder not to behave the way I did back in high school, all of those years ago.

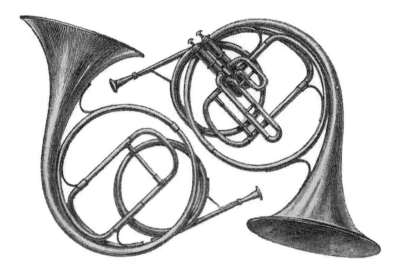

I ALWAYS LIKED JEWS

Back before I spent the year in Edinburgh, my great uncle—who was my grandmother's younger brother, and was childless by choice—decided to take me out for lunch to convince me not to marry Fiona since she wasn't Jewish. He took me out to lunch at one of the restaurants that his "buddies" probably felt was a pretty fancy place. It was horrendous. The food was not memorable, but the décor was unforgettable.

It was gaudy. There were statues of old knights and plastic flowers. There was a huge chandelier in the middle, and a large staircase that went up to the second floor. They put a grand piano in the middle, under the chandelier. We sat on the top floor in an exclusive area, as practically the only people eating lunch that day in the restaurant. Since I had never been taken out for lunch by my great uncle before, this was quite a special occasion. He didn't tell me what the meal was about before we started. After a few niceties, he got straight into business.

He asked me if it was my intention to marry Fiona. I was thinking about it seriously. He told me that, of all of his grand nieces and nephews, I was the one he felt was most likely to live a Jewish life. How could I possibly marry a non-Jew? He just could not understand it. For me it was a matter of love and had nothing to do with my upbringing or my principles.

There were already cracks in our relationship before I decided to go to Edinburgh. Fiona and I spoke about how we would raise our children. I wanted to raise them as Jews; I didn't realize back then that my children would not be Jewish if they were born to a non-Jewish woman. But that was irrelevant to me at the time. I told her that, if we had a son, I would want him to be circumcised. I still hadn't been to Scotland and I didn't realize that Scottish men on the whole were not circumcised. This was an abomination to her. She told me there was absolutely no way that her son was going to be circumcised.

I even had a conversation with Fiona's mother and she said, "I always liked Jews. I have nothing against the Jewish people." I know it wasn't coming from a place of being anti-Jewish. It was coming from a place of not being comfortable with what I was comfortable with. It brought home to me that I really shouldn't be married to this woman, but I was so in love that I couldn't think rationally.

My great uncle decided to tell me a little bit about himself in order to convince me not to marry Fiona. He grew up in an Orthodox Jewish home. They were proud Jews and everyone in the family married a Jew. He reminded me how I grew up, being a proud Jew, and asked how I could possibly marry this woman.

But here we were, sitting in a non-kosher restaurant. My uncle was not religious by any means. He never had any children of his own, by his own choice, and he didn't keep *Shabbos*. I thought to myself, who is this guy to tell me what I should be doing? What kind of a role model is he?

I asked my great uncle when he stopped being religious and why. He did not hesitate, and told me straight out. He said that when he was in his late teens, around seventeen or eighteen, he and his older brother were traveling salesmen. He recalled the first time that he was on the train and put on *tefillin*. Everyone on the train stared at him like he was a freak. He was so embarrassed that he put his *tallis* and *tefillin* away and never put them on again, ever.

I asked him, "What kind of role model are you?" He told me that he didn't want me to make the same mistakes that he made in his life, then admitted it was true that he and his wife could have had children, but they chose not to. However, he had made many mistakes, and it would be a great mistake for me to marry Fiona.

The conversation was relatively short before I told him that I didn't feel like he was the right person to be telling me what to do with my life. We finished our meal and went our separate ways, until the next family occasion brought us together.

My uncle passed away decades ago now, but I still remember our conversation together. It wasn't because of him that I ultimately did not marry Fiona, but he was right. I respect the fact that it meant so much to him that he was willing to take the risk of asking me to change my life, even though he himself did not have the guts to change his own. It was his own personal redemption.

The truth is, you can't live vicariously through someone else. If you make mistakes, fix what you can. Give advice, if you really think it will help and you think the person that you're giving it to will accept it. But remember, it's never too late to change your own life, even if it's just for a short moment. It's never too late.

TEFILLIN WITH NO HANDS

I've been living in Jerusalem, Israel for over twenty years now. Unfortunately, I've seen my share of terrorism. My psychological wounds are internal, but I've seen many people with external wounds from the terror and wars we've been through. There were four people that I remember well.

The first was a guy missing both of his legs. He was in an electric wheelchair. I'd see him in the Shuk area. I don't know what happened to him, but I'm guessing it was either a terrorist attack or an injury from the army. His legs were amputated at his mid-thighs, he grew his hair long and had a wild beard to go with his wild hair. I've seen guys like this before, but older; he was maybe in his late twenties.

These guys are pissed off. They're pissed off at the people who talk with them, and they're pissed off at the whole world. I remember this guy well, because he used to dart out fast into moving traffic with his electric wheelchair, almost tempting drivers to hit him. When the cars or buses would screech to a halt and the drivers would scream at this guy, he'd just have a smile on his face that said, "F*** you, a**holes." I watched this happen so many times I lost count.

After a while he disappeared from the Shuk area and I actually saw him again in another busy part of town, playing the same game with traffic and giving the same satisfied smile after he nearly messed up someone's car. I thought about him a lot, trying to figure out how I could help him. I started saying "shalom" to him whenever I saw him and tried to stop traffic when I could so he could cross the street. He never spoke with me, and that was the end of my relationship with him. Eventually he moved locations and I stopped seeing him altogether.

Soon after my move to Jerusalem, I got to know some of the beggars since I wanted to help them. They weren't joking when they said they were homeless. They had really hard lives. Not all of them, of course, but the ones that passed away certainly did.

There was one guy whose name I never learned. We were pretty friendly back in the old days. He had one leg and got around on a pair of crutches. He was older, dirty, and looked like he hadn't had a shower since 1973, when he lost his leg in the Yom Kippur war. That much I had learned from him. He had a tin box that he'd collect money in. He would stand on the main pedestrian street, Ben Yehuda, collecting money for hours every day while resting his stump on an old, dirty wooden crutch.

One day I was on the bus to Tel Aviv and I saw the legless, crutch-carrying war veteran. "Hey," I said to him, "what are you doing here?" as if he could never leave Ben Yehuda street.

"I have a gig in Tel Aviv too," he said.

"What?" I was astounded.

He smiled and said, "What did you think? I only work the streets in Jerusalem? People have money in Tel Aviv too." I never imagined he worked more than one city.

There was a little sandwich shop on the ground floor of the building where I used to get my lunch daily. That place is gone now, replaced by another sandwich shop that's also now gone. It was right next to the main entrance.

One day, while waiting in line to get a sandwich, a blind guy with a guide stick came storming past security. He was banging his stick back and forth like he was trying to move everything out of his way rather than guide himself. His stick was practically a weapon; he was pissed off at everyone around him and seemed pissed off at the whole world. I know from the woman who worked at the sandwich shop that he had lost his vision just a year before, from an explosion that a terrorist set off.

As he came down the stairs to the sandwich shop with his guide stick/weapon, those of us in line moved aside to avoid being injured. The blind guy came over to the sandwich stand yelling that he needed a sandwich right now. The woman making the sandwiches had a lot of compassion for this guy. She told him to sit down and she would take care of him in order, but he pretended as if he didn't hear her.

"Shoshi," he said, "I need my sandwich now!"

"Sit down and wait," said Shoshi, "there are other people in front of you." Those of us in line were more than happy to let the blind guy get his sandwich first and leave us in peace, but Shoshi wasn't. I insisted that the blind guy go ahead of me. Shoshi obliged. The blind guy didn't say anything. I could sense he wanted to say "thank you," but he wasn't ready for such kind words.

Shoshi and I would talk about him after he left. We pitied him for being so bitter. It's a terrible thing to lose your vision, especially to a terrorist. I understand. But what are you going to do? The only choice we have is to move on.

The last person in my group of four people who made a huge impact on me is someone I think about almost every day. We never said a word to one another. I simply didn't have the guts to speak with him, but his presence changed my perspective on life. I *daven* in the same shul every week day, where I always sit in the same corner. Normally I lead the *davening*, so I stand in the front of the shul with my back to everyone.

One morning, as I was putting on my *tefillin*, a guy in his late forties or early fifties came into the shul. He had no hands, only two prosthetic arms with hooks. That was shocking enough, but then he took out his *tefillin* and started putting them on with his prosthetics.

Tefillin are long leather straps connected to two hard leather boxes. You put one box on your upper arm, and then wrap the strap around the lower portion of your arm. The other one goes on your head like a headband with the box in the middle, above your forehead. It's not easy to put on *tefillin* with arms and hands, but to see someone put them on with prosthetic arms blew me away.

He took the *tefillin* out of their bag, then pushed up his sleeve revealing that he had upper arms. With grace and skill honed over the years, he quickly put the arm *tefillin* on his left arm. Then he circled his left arm in the air while the strap wrapped around his prosthetic limb. Afterward he took the head *tefillin* and, with his hooks, put it on his head as naturally as would anyone with hands. He opened his *siddur* (prayer book) and started *davening* with the rest of us. Everyone in shul was staring at the guy. We were totally captivated by him. He was just like the rest of us and treated his hooks like hands as if it was no big deal.

He came back again the next day, and the day after. Every day I stared at him. I couldn't help myself. I wasn't staring at him because he had no hands, but was watching how he was able to overcome his injuries. A lot of people would have abandoned God, having lost both of their hands, but not this guy. This was at least four or five years ago. I still look over to where he was standing those three mornings and imagine him there putting on *tefillin* with no hands.

A year or so later, he was written up in *Sichat Hashavua*, the weekly newsletter of the Chabad movement in Israel. It turns out that his hands were blown up in a work accident. After he had recovered from his injury, this amazing man founded a non-profit organization to feed Jews who couldn't put food on the table. This man is unstoppable.

I'm sure he has his bad days. Somehow, I'm not really sure how, he made peace with and overcame his trauma. He wasn't bitter, he wasn't violent and he didn't want compassion. He moved forward. He moved upward. He made the most of what he has. And that's why I admire him.

PINCHAS WAS A ZEALOT

I *daven* in an interesting shul. It's a totally Haredi (isolationist Orthodox), Yiddish speaking shul that wouldn't have a *minyan* if it weren't for the non-Haredi *chevre* (guys) that also *daven* there, like me. They're exposed to us, and we to them. There are two main characters in the shul. One leads the *minyan* before mine. The other is always late and scrapes together a *minyan* of stragglers. They have similar names but very different personalities.

One is named Pesach Simcha but he only uses the name Simcha. The other is named Simcha Pinchas, but he never uses the name Simcha. Simcha means "joy" or "happiness." Pinchas was the zealot in the Torah who put a spear through the genitals of a Jewish man having relations with an idol-worshiping prostitute. Both are popular names in the Jewish world. It's much nicer to name your child Simcha (happiness) than Pinchas (the zealot).

We gave Pinchas the nickname "the drill sergeant," since he talks out of the side of his mouth and everything he says is like a command. I've never seen him smile and he's always in a bad mood. Maybe his parents had a premonition when they named him Pinchas. If so, they were right. The least they could do was add the name "happiness," even though he never seems happy. Unfortunately for those around him, the name he chooses to go by fits Pinchas much better than his first name, Simcha.

The other fellow, similar in age and even in build, only goes by the name Simcha. I didn't even know his first name was Pesach until recently, and I've known him for many years. Simcha is always *b'simcha* (happy). He's one of the happiest people I know. He's one of my role models. Both of these gentlemen are grandfathers and probably great grandfathers. They're both overweight and I've never seen Pinchas smoke, but Simcha used to smoke so much that it's physically hard for him to get around now.

I've seen Simcha in the *mikva* (ritual pool). It's a labor for him to get dressed, especially putting on his socks, but he does it one step at a time, with lots of breaks in-between. The whole time he smiles, as if to say to Hashem, "You're making this hard for me, but I can handle it."

I realized only recently that they both share the name Simcha, but that one chooses to be happy and the other chooses to be a zealot. How powerful our choices are.

An amazing thing happened the other day. I saw Pinchas in shul. He came over to me smiling. I don't think I've ever seen his teeth in the nearly twenty years I've known him. It was so beautiful to see Pinchas smiling. He grumbled out of the side of his mouth, "Here, take this," handing me an invitation to his daughter's wedding. It was the last child he was marrying off, and he was so happy I hardly recognized him.

It turned out that he only gave me the invitation the day before the wedding and by mistake I missed it. I saw him in shul the day after with his new son-in-law. Pinchas was shining, happier than I'd ever seen him. His new son-in-law must have thought Pinchas was always a happy man, since he was glowing the whole time his arm was around him. I blessed Pinchas that he should always be at least as happy as he was that day, and only happier and happier all the time. He answered with a loud "Amen!"

A few months after the wedding he was still smiling. There was a sense of satisfaction about him, like after marrying off his daughter he'd finally made it in life. I shook his hand and he smiled, which made me smile even more. How powerful are the choices we make in life. Sometimes, not always, but when we are able, we can choose to be happy, like Simcha and Pinchas.

IT WORRIES MY
MOTHER-IN-LAW

I talk to myself all the time. It's not such a big deal really because, with modern cell phones, everyone looks like they're talking to themselves. My mother-in-law once caught me talking to myself and was very upset. She kept telling me to stop. I think she was genuinely worried that I might be crazy.

I ask myself multiple times a day, usually looking into the mirror, "What's going on, Barak? What are you doing? What's happening? Talk to me." Of course, I know what's going on but, when I verbalize it, it's easier to handle. Sometimes I'll tell myself that things are going great and remind myself that there's nothing to complain about. Other times I'll try to figure out what I should be doing right now. Sometimes it's a short list, like, "start this online advertising campaign, finish that task and then go buy lunch." Other times it's more focused like, "take a shower, brush your teeth and go to sleep." It keeps me in line. When I feel like things are getting out of control, talking to myself always helps.

Sometimes I need to be my own therapist. I'll ask myself, "What's bothering me?" If it's something specific, I'll actually talk it out. I'll say something like, "That S.O.B. called me a what? I can't believe he said that! Why would he say that to me? Maybe I am a little of what he said? I don't know. I don't want to see him again, that's for sure. But what are you going to do next time you see him? Should I remain silent or tell him off? I'm not sure. Let's think about this a little and try to sort it out right now before I see him again." I'll go on like that until I come up with a decision of what I should do.

When I'm at work, alone in my office, I talk out loud. I make jokes. I curse. I laugh. I say what I should be doing now. I remind myself to focus, "Focus, Barak, focus," and then get back to work.

I know it sounds a little crazy to some people, like my mother-in-law, but the truth is, talking to myself has always been a lifesaver. It's what keeps me sane.

I'M HERE NOW

A few days before I left to drive up to North Carolina to work at the Boy Scout camp (and then afterward to drive up to New Jersey to attend Rutgers) I stopped in a pizza chain to get something to eat. It was just a place I passed on my way to somewhere. I don't even remember why I was there, but I do remember seeing my friend, Daryl, working there. Daryl and I had been in a marching band together. I was the head of the entire brass section and knew everyone in the band. We spent a lot of time together in practices and at games.

My high school was integrated with blacks, whites and Hispanics from all parts of Miami. I drove a lot of the black guys home after the football games to where they lived in the poorest sections of Miami. There were no buses that late at night. I knew where Daryl lived and I knew he was poor.

There Daryl was, in a uniform, standing behind the counter. I asked him how he was doing. What's going on? What's he doing with his life now that we're a year past high school? He said, "I'm here now." In my mind it was clear that he was in community college, like I was, working in the pizza place to make ends meet while he was getting an education and making exciting plans like me. But was I was wrong.

When I asked him how community college was going, he said he tried for a little bit, but it wasn't for him. So, I figured he was working on something else on the side, maybe a business? Maybe he was training to be a manager or buy his own franchise. Again I was wrong. When Daryl said, "I'm here now," he didn't mean, "I'm here *for* now," he meant that he was *there now* and that's it. No other plans. When I asked if he had anything else in mind besides this job, he said "No. I'm here now."

I left South Florida a few days later and I haven't looked back since. We can only see as far as our minds will allow us. A friend of mine likes to say "Argue for your limitations and they're yours." How many times do we not even know that we're limiting ourselves? I'm pretty sure Daryl has moved on to bigger and better things by now.

I had an English teacher in high school that made a real impact on my life by saying one small thing. Without knowing it, I was in an experimental school. This teacher's class was held in an auditorium with three teachers teaching at the same time, one right after the other, trying to keep our attention. They would teach us some poem or piece of literature and then ask us to write something on a specific topic. We'd hand in our papers, they'd grade them on the spot and call us down to the bottom of the auditorium to give us their feedback. One teacher called me to come closer to her. She said, "You're going to be a success in life, not because you're so great, but because everyone else is so bad."

What a thing to tell a kid. That was so many years ago, but I kept it in mind all this time and, you know what? She was right. There were times when I really doubted myself, but her words kept me from falling too low. I looked around me and realized that, even though I wasn't so great at that moment, compared to everyone else, I was doing really well, and that helped me to not give up.

THE OLD GUY FROM RUSSIA WITHOUT KIDS

I judge people quickly and usually unfairly. As a result, I've tried to cultivate the habit of finding something positive in every situation or person. So I can at least try to judge them positively.

There's a guy that comes very occasionally to my *minyan* in shul. He has no patience for me; I *daven* slow and wait for the latecomers to catch up in the *davening*. Most of the people that come to the *minyan* know this. But this guy doesn't, and he really doesn't care. He's got a schedule to keep, places to go. I'm not exactly sure where he's going, but I do know that he's very anxious to get there. He either tries to start the *davening* before I do, or is constantly pushing me to go faster and faster.

He doesn't care that I don't want to *daven* fast and I've lost my patience for him over time. Internally I made fun of him: how he looks, how he talks, walks and acts. I could entertain myself regularly making fun of this guy, oftentimes causing myself to laugh out loud without anyone else knowing why.

One day, he came and said *kaddish*. Then a few days later he's back saying *kaddish* again. Over the next year, he came every now and then, once every few months, and said *kaddish* for someone. I guessed one of his parents had passed away. When the year of saying *kaddish* is over, usually the person who lost a loved one makes a little kiddish where we all have a cookie or piece of cake and say "*l'chaim*" to the soul that left this world. This guy finished the year and made his *l'chaim*.

I asked him who he was saying *kaddish* for, and he said "Levy." "Levy who?" I asked. "Levy, you know the old guy from Russia who didn't have any kids to say *kaddish* for him?" Oh my God, I said to myself, he had been saying *kaddish* for Levy? I knew who Levy was, but I didn't know much about him.

He was an old guy who could hardly see. He used a huge magnifying glass to read the *siddur* as he *daven*ed. You couldn't miss him. He was a sight to behold and came to the shul where I *daven* for *mincha* on *Shabbos* (a different shul from my weekday *minyan*) and was given the Levite *aliyah*. His name was Levy and he was a Levite.

He came up to the Torah with a *siddur* and his giant magnifying glass. I thought it was so strange. For sure he knew the blessing you say when you're called up to the Torah by heart, but he brought the *siddur* and the magnifying glass. The next *Shabbos* the rabbi of the shul, Rav Segal, gave a whole talk about Levy and how he passed away about an hour after that *aliyah* to the Torah. It made a real impact on me.

Here we were, *davening* together on *Shabbos* afternoon, and one of Levy's last acts in this world was being called up to the Torah. This was the Levy that the guy who I made fun of was saying *kaddish* for. Oy vey. How could I make fun of this guy? He's amazing. He's been saying *kaddish* for a whole year for Levy and I've been making fun of him?

I still judge people quickly, but now I always, always force myself to find something positive about them to focus on so I don't make the same mistake again. When you find something good in others, you're doing it by means of finding something good in yourself, just like the guy who said *kaddish* for Levy.

SAY THAT AGAIN
AND I'LL KILL YOU

When I was in high school, I wanted to be cool and popular like everyone else but, at some point, quite early on, I realized that I wasn't one of the popular kids. I had plenty of friends, but that "popular kid" thing wasn't going to be me.

I wanted to like certain music (which I didn't) because everyone else did. I wanted to dress in a "cool" way and have an image; a look. I wore all kinds of clothes I didn't like and had a trendy haircut that I didn't like either. I felt that I was supposed to be a certain type of person that I also didn't like. In short, I had no idea what I really liked and was just trying to make other people happy. I figured I would be happy when I had the acceptance of people that I admired.

Later on, in my last year of high school, I fully embraced who I really was. All of a sudden, I became very popular. When I made an effort toward being trendy and cool, I wasn't. But when I gave up on it entirely and just embraced who I really am, I became cool—unintentionally, of course.

I went on a semester program in Israel in my last year of high school and came back a changed person. My band teacher had said, "Good kids go to that program in Israel and come back as bad kids." I was always such a good kid: well behaved, quiet, and never caused trouble. I thought, that might happen to other kids who went on the Israel program, but that would never happen to me. But it did, and boy did I become a rebel.

I didn't change who I was on the inside, I just got in touch with it. My rebellion started in economics class. For years I had sat in school listening to teachers that were too bored with their lives to care or teachers with an agenda to make their students think like them. But I never had the guts to stand up to my teachers. I had never even thought to stand up to a teacher. What was the point? But now I couldn't help myself.

The economics teacher gave us an exercise. We were to start with a thousand dollars, pick some stocks, and track them for the next week. I was happy to learn about trading stocks, but there was one kid who either wasn't interested or did the exercise wrong and the teacher ripped into him. I watched this and felt like this kid needed someone to stand up for him.

I made a comment to the teacher, quietly, to leave the kid alone. The teacher then looked at me, in shock, and basically told me to shut my mouth. After hardly saying a word the entire year, I then ripped into this teacher like no student ever should. He sat down stunned. The class gave me a standing ovation. He then told me, "If you're so smart, get up and teach the rest of the class," so I did.

It was exhilarating; a thrill like I'd never experienced in my life. It was a rush of adrenaline and, in a split second, I became a popular kid. The funny thing is that, at that point in my life, I really didn't care. I actually hated popular kids. They were fakes and I told them straight to their faces. I pretty much told everyone what I thought straight to their face. So many people were disturbed by my behavior; most of the time they didn't know how to react. For me nothing had changed. I always had these thoughts and imagined myself telling people what I really thought, but I was too scared and shy to say anything. I simply took what was inside of me and put some of it on the outside. Then the floodgates had opened. Poor teachers. While the kids in the school loved what I had become, the teachers didn't know how to react.

My parents had the good wisdom to force me to take a yearlong typing class. It's thanks to that class that I know how to type this book that I'm writing now. There were no computers back then except for these big, bulky IBMs with green screens. We used typewriters. They were electric, and they were big machines. You would type a letter and the whole table would shake from the power of the typewriter.

Keeping us from talking during class wasn't a problem since when all fifty of us started typing you couldn't hear anything else. The teacher was bored with her job and who could blame her? After we all learned to type the goal became to type as fast as possible. So this teacher would give us articles from the encyclopedia to type and, since she was Black, she liked for us to type about famous Black people.

The teacher would hand out the typing assignment and then sit at the front of the class reading a magazine waiting for us to finish. After spending a couple of months writing articles about famous Americans, mainly Black ones, the teacher announced, "This month is Black History Month and the entire month we'll be typing about famous Black Americans." I could not believe it. How many famous Black Americans can there be?

After about a week of typing about Black Americans, I asked the teacher when we were going to type about famous Jewish Americans. She told me to sit down, shut up and type. This went on for a while—me asking her to write about Jewish Americans and the teacher telling me where I could put my request.

At the end of Black History Month, I decided to photocopy an article about Albert Einstein and put a copy on everyone's desk before the class started. When the students arrived, they knew exactly who was responsible. Everyone knew I had been trying to get the subject of the articles changed without success.

When the typing teacher came in and gave us yet another article about slavery or a famous Black American, I spoke up, saying, "Maybe today we could type about Albert Einstein?" I said I had photocopied the articles and already distributed them to the other students. The teacher was beside herself. She shouted for everyone to bring her the "illegal photocopies," threw them in the garbage, and then sent me to the principal.

The principal was a nice Black woman who had a publicly known drinking problem. I had been sent to her before for rebelling in class. When I walked in this time, she said to me, "What now?" I told her how we had spent a whole month, and practically the whole year, typing about famous Black Americans, but had ignored the Jewish population. I had photocopied articles about Albert Einstein and handed them out to the class, and that was why I was there. Of course, she had no problem with us writing about famous Black people and slavery, but when I mentioned the Jews she got very angry.

There was an entire month for Black awareness and not even one day for Jewish awareness? "When are we going to type articles about Jews?" I asked.

She answered, "The Jews were never slaves like my people were."

I looked at her in dismay. "Never slaves?" I said, "Have you ever heard of the Bible? There's a whole section there that talks about how the Jews were slaves in Egypt. And what about the Nazis? Have you heard of them? They also enslaved the Jews. So did the Romans. Have you—?" She cut me off there and said to just sit in the secretary's office until the hour was over, and then go to the next class.

She said, "Don't come back here. I really don't want to see you anymore."

But it didn't take long for me to be back. This time it was a whole new level of rebellion. Our school was supposed to be a model of integration. While it was located in a predominantly white and Jewish neighborhood, the school was one-third white, one-third black and one-third Hispanic. The black and Hispanic kids were bused in from far away.

There were kids with knives and kids that sold drugs in our sweet little school of three thousand students. We all knew who they were. One of the thugs, who was Jamaican, was in our typing class. He didn't like my insisting that we type about Jews when he thought we should be typing about blacks. We were in class one day and he came over to my table, leaned in close and said in his Jamaican accent, "You gotta problem with da black man?"

I looked up at him and said, "No. Do you?"

He smiled slowly and said, "You're dead. Just wait until after class."

The whole rest of the class I was trying to figure out what to do. I had a car. I could just leave school and go to work early, or I could go to the teacher and tell her. I could tell my friends to try to protect me maybe, but I really didn't know what to do. I decided to tell the teacher that this kid threatened to beat me up after class. She told me to sit down, shut up and type. I sat there the whole hour nervously typing, not sure what to do or what I had gotten myself into. When class was over, I decided to just ignore it. He wasn't serious, right? We were in 12th grade. Who got into fights anymore?

It turns out I was wrong. I had just walked out of class when this thug came over to me, grabbed my shoulder and asked me again if I had a problem with black people. My adrenaline was rushing now. I asked him, "Do you have a problem with Jewish people?" At this point, a circle of students had surrounded us and were shouting "Fight! Fight! Fight!"

I looked around me. No one was going to save me, not my friends nor the teachers, who weren't even present. This guy could not believe I had the guts to talk back to him. He said to me, "Say that again and I'll kill you."

My grandfather grew up as an immigrant kid in America. He got beat up a lot as a kid, until he learned to fight. He always told me I needed to know how to fight, "Just in case." To make sure I had a chance, he bought me a full-sized, professional punching bag when I was thirteen and insisted I use it every day. I had hit that punching bag every single night for the previous five years. So when I punched the Jamaican as hard as I could in the face, it knocked him on the floor. By the time he got up, the teachers had showed up and pulled him away before he had a chance to touch me.

He was taken away and I was sent to the principal's office. "What did you do now?" the principal asked. The teachers showed up to tell her what had happened. Then she turned to me, "We've been trying to get that kid kicked out of this school the entire year," she said, with a smile. "You're suspended for the day. Go. Get out of here."

As I left the principal's office, I could see students staring at me.

Eventually one of my friends came over to me and told me I was awesome. "I can't believe what you just did," he said. It turns out that a lot of other students felt the same way. The teachers found drugs and a knife on the student and he was finally kicked out of school. I never had any problems with him again.

I instantly became one of the most popular kids in school, but I didn't realize it. There were only a few more weeks left of high school at that point. The last couple of days, kids started writing in each other's yearbooks. A friend of mine was writing his farewells in my yearbook when one of the most popular girls in school asked my friend to give her the yearbook. We both looked at each other amazed while she wrote.

I don't think she and I had ever spoken with each other all of the years we were in school together. She wrote what she wanted, then kissed the page, leaving a lipstick mark. She gave the yearbook back to me, and walked away with a smile, staring at me as she left.

My friend and I quickly opened the yearbook to see what she wrote. It said, "Barak, why didn't you ask me out?" with a lipstick kiss on my name. My friend and I looked at each other, "What?" We could not believe what we just saw.

This happened over and over during the last two days of school. All kinds of kids were asking to write in my yearbook. Boys would write that I was their hero and they wished they could be more like me. The girls said, "I wished you had asked me out." Oh my God, this was happening right before my eyes and I had no idea. I had become a cool, popular kid and didn't know until the last two days of high school!

There's a joke about an Orthodox rabbi who gets a hole in one on the golf course on Yom Kippur and can't tell anyone about it because he's not supposed to be golfing on the holiest day of the year. That was kind of like my last two days of high school. I was such a poor student all of my years of school that no university would accept me. All of my friends went off to their futures at Harvard and Princeton or to the Marines and I was stuck at home with my parents, on my way to community college.

Even though it felt like I became the person I had always strived to be in high school, it was never something that could last for the rest of my life. The only thing that I would really take from that last year was the self confidence I found. That same self confidence has carried me to today. One of the reasons I could tap into it was because I finally didn't worry what other people thought about me.

THE WINDOW AT HABA

I am writing this book in a restaurant near the Shuk and the train tracks in Jerusalem. They know that I come here every week at the same time to write. So the restaurant management gives me a quiet place to work. From my table on the second floor, I can see the street through half of a huge bay window.

Outside the window, people pass by in a steady stream of life. I see them for literally two or three seconds, and most of them I'll never see again. I see the homeless and the religious, the young and the beautiful, the old and weathered, natives and tourists. Every person has their story. Every person is a world.

They can't see me, but I can see them. When I look closely I can tap into their lives for a second and then it passes. I feel their love and passion for a second, and then sometimes their sadness and depression for the next. It's like living a hundred lifetimes, each of them a few seconds long.

AN ENTIRE BOTTLE
OF VODKA

Purim is a funny holiday. Most people don't get Purim. I certainly didn't get it for years. It actually got to the point where I treated Purim like a minor holiday. That is, I pretty much ignored it. Then one day, I heard it said in the Zohar that Yom Kippur, considered the absolute holiest day of the Jewish year, is really called Yom Kep-Purim, meaning the "Day of Atonement," the day "like Purim." For the longest time I didn't understand it. How could Purim, a day on which many people dress in costumes, get drunk and act silly, possibly be like Yom Kippur, the most sacred day of the year? I knew I was missing something.

For starters, I almost never drink, and certainly never get drunk. But after reading in a book about the laws of Purim—which said that a person should consume as much alcohol as he possibly can— I decided that I would at least drink a little on Purim. The *mitzvah* is to get drunk "*ad de lo yada*" ("until one doesn't know the difference").

This means, until the point that you don't know the difference between "Blessed is Mordechai" and "Cursed is Haman." For many people, it means getting drunk during the day, not at night. Some rabbis, notably the Rambam, say that this means you need to drink until you've fallen asleep (or just fall asleep without drinking). When you're sleeping you don't know the difference between blessed is Mordechai and cursed is Haman. But I knew there had to be more to this and I was determined to figure it out.

I started with taking the costumes seriously. Every year I would take my kids to buy costumes and one year I decided to buy one for myself. It was a clown suit. It was really made for big kids, but back then I was thinner and could fit into it. Then I made a decision that, any time someone would offer me a drink on Purim, I would drink with them. The first time I did this I actually got drunk. I didn't fall asleep and I could still tell you that Mordechai was the hero and Haman was the villain, but I did have a lot of fun.

The next year, I got drunk at night. I really didn't mean to. If you don't drink often, you don't have a feel for how much you need to drink before you get drunk. I had no clue. I followed my policy of: if you offer me a drink, I'll drink with you. Before I knew it, I was drunk.

I was at a party at shul that night and, when the party ended, I came home drunk. It wasn't raging drunk; it was silly drunk. I was sitting on the steps at the entrance to our house telling my wife I needed another party to go to that night. It was already past 9 pm. There had to be a party somewhere. She said that there was a megillah reading at a neighbor's house. Before she finished the sentence, I was stumbling my way toward the neighbor.

I knocked on the door and walked in. The house was hot from all the people crowded inside and my glasses steamed up immediately. I was still in the clown costume, trying to figure out what do I do now. It wasn't a party.

It was a very quiet, civil reading of the megillah. Here's the thing about the megillah: when you reach Haman's name, you are supposed to make a racket and blot it out. Some people have groggers (noise makers), whistles, or drums; some shout "boo" or just stomp their feet on the floor. The reader there read the name "Haman" and there was a little rumble of boos and some feet shuffling. I thought to myself, what is this? This is crazy. It's Purim and this is how a group of Jews is behaving? They need a clown to wake them up! The next time Haman's name was read, I went crazy shouting "boo," jumping up and down, flailing my arms in the air, shouting "yuck, yuck," and basically doing anything I could think of to make noise.

The civilized crowd was offended. Some people even said, "Barak, please, not so loud." My answer? "Not so loud? Not so loud! Wait until they mention *that guy's* name again." I just waited for the reader to say Haman's name. Of course he did, and I went even crazier than before. I took chairs and shoved them while I jumped up and down screaming boos and yuck yucks.

The subdued crowd had no patience for me. I was warned to calm down or I'd be asked to leave. After the third time, I was forcibly escorted out the door from which I entered. I thought to myself, "Man, that was fun. Where can I go now?" But I didn't find any more parties or megillah readings that year. I couldn't get drunk during the day. That was the end of my drinking for the year, but I had discovered something. I didn't yet know what it was, but there was something special about Purim that I reached through my once a year drinking. It required further exploration.

The next year, we were invited to a daytime Purim meal hosted by friends who had moved to Israel from America. I brought a full bottle of vodka with me to share with everyone at the meal. It was a nice group of civilized people. There was one family with a mentally and physically underdeveloped son. There was also a well-known rabbi there who had recently moved from the States.

He told me his name used to be Reb Chaim of Minnesota (or something like that) and, now that he was living in Jerusalem, he called himself "Reb Chaim of Yerushalayim" (of Jerusalem). He said he came from a long line of Chassidic rebbes and rabbis. He had a period where he stopped being religious and, now that he was religious again, he wanted to help bring Jews closer to Judaism. He was a sweet man.

After the meal had started, I began walking around from table to table offering people "*l'chaims*." Some people would have a little sip of the vodka, but most refused to drink even a drop. So, out of the kindness of my soul, I offered to drink their *l'chaim* for them. After a few hours, I had finished the bottle, mostly by myself. Wow, I thought to myself, this is a first. I wonder what's going to happen now? Unfortunately, I don't remember everything that happened, but I can recall short moments of the day and the meal.

It's kind of like going on a merry-go-round and trying to remember all of the people that passed by, maybe a little clearer. All of sudden, I could only see the good in everyone. There's a saying that "When the wine goes in, the secret comes out" (Babylonian Talmud, *Eruv*in 65a). I guess it was a good sign for me if seeing the good in everyone was the secret brought out by the vodka.

I started going around the room, from table to table, telling everyone good things about themselves. I would tell the husbands good things about their wives and the wives good things about their husbands. To the parents I would say good things about their kids. Everyone was a bit astonished, because I was both right and entertaining. They were laughing, while I was having the time of my life, and to think that this was a *mitzvah*.

Then I went over to Reb Chaim of Yerushalayim and a strange

thing happened. I didn't see any good in him. It was like sound-can-celling headphones: you expect to hear something, but it's silent. Then I thought, maybe I would look for something bad in him, but I didn't see anything bad in him at all. This was so strange. I could see the good in everyone like it was a neon light over their heads but, with Reb Chaim, all I saw was his *shtreimel*. I told him I couldn't see anything and just gave him a blessing, that he should be successful in all of his efforts to bring good into this world. Reb Chaim has since passed away. He died at fifty-two, having brought thousands of Jews closer to Judaism.

I met a great rabbi many years later, Rabbi Adin Steinsaltz. I expected to see lightning coming out of this great *tzadik*, but when I stood next to him I felt nothing. It was like Reb Chaim, but even more so. When you stand next to Rabbi Steinsaltz—which I have, many times at this point—you feel nothing. I realized that's a true *tzadik*; humility. Reb Chaim was the same.

Then I made my way over to the mentally retarded boy. He was so happy to see me. I was wearing a clown suit, after all. He was smiling and seemed to be happy all the time. I loved this kid. Somehow, I could see something in him that I hadn't seen before I got drunk. This kid was shining. The sparks that I hoped to see from Reb Chaim, I saw in this kid.

I asked the boy to give me a *dvar Torah* (share some Torah related thoughts with me), and everything that came out of his mouth blew me away. I asked his parents if they understood what a special, holy soul their son was, but they had this worried look on their faces like they were concerned I would do something stupid. I didn't. I just hugged and kissed him and asked him to tell me more words of Torah. I hung out with him until the party was over. I couldn't get enough of him.

There's a little problem when you drink an entire bottle of vodka and the party ends. It ends for everyone else, but not for you. My wife said she was taking the kids home and to be careful. I told her I'm going to my friend Allon's house. For sure the party is still going there. I did make it to Allon's house, which was a fifteen-minute walk from the first party, but I have no idea what happened after I got there. The day ended... and I didn't drink again until next Purim.

The next Purim, my poor father was visiting. He got to experience his son, who he loves and respects, get totally drunk, vomit and nearly pass out. It wasn't my intention at all. I figured if I could drink a whole bottle of vodka the previous year, I could do it again this year.

I bought a bottle of vodka and started drinking a cup at a time at eleven in the morning. My father told me to take it slow, but I didn't feel anything. I figured, maybe I have some Russian blood. My family lived for generations in exile in Russia before moving to America. How else could I drink an entire bottle of vodka the previous year and not feel anything? With this in mind, I decided I would take the kids to hand out the *mishlochey manot* (food gifts Jews give each other on Purim). I usually prepare a hundred and hand them all out. It's a lot of fun... usually.

I was wearing my clown costume and the vodka still hadn't hit me. My kids and I started going from home to home handing out the gifts. Then I started to feel something; a little buzz. I was happy. I was making jokes. The kids were having fun. Then it hit me like a Mac truck. It was like jumping into the water. Everything slowed down and sped up at the same time. It was horrible. I didn't know what was happening to me. If I were on a bus, I would have gotten off. But with vodka, there's no getting off.

I started throwing up. I told my oldest daughter to take the younger kids home while I continued to throw up. When I got home, I apologized to my family and then went to sleep, waking up occasionally to throw up in a bucket which my wife had put near our bed. When I finally got the vodka out of my system, I realized that drinking itself wasn't the secret of Purim. All I did was get drunk. I didn't have any revelations. I didn't even enjoy myself.

The next year came, and this time I figured that if I only drink half a bottle of vodka I'd be in better shape. I marked the bottle at the halfway point with a red marker and started drinking slowly. It worked much better. I got a little drunk. I didn't get sick. I always wanted to hug people but felt uncomfortable. It wasn't me, but sometimes I just wanted to hug my friends and wouldn't let myself.

That Purim a friend came by my house and the first thing I did was run over to him and hug him. He hugged me back. Then I started hugging every male friend that came by the house. I realized that, when I'm drunk, I can do things I wouldn't allow myself otherwise. Since other people were also drunk, intending to get drunk or at least expecting drunk behavior, they also didn't mind.

I thought about how I could use the Purim atmosphere effectively. I have these neighbors that, at least at some point, were small time gangsters. When we moved into our neighborhood of Nachlaot in the mid-1990s, it was still a neighborhood in transition. Once a glorious area of town, it had become a slum. It had drug dealers, prostitutes and criminals; it also had the young folks like my wife and me.

A few doors from our house was the family of gangsters. Across the street was a drug dealer, and one street away was a religious pimp with his prostitutes, more drug dealers and junkies. It was a bad scene.

We once had a new neighbor who was living in the house we share a wall with. They had moved from Tel Aviv to the hip, gentrifying Nachlaot of Jerusalem. My gangster neighbors made some comment about how hot this guy's girlfriend was, and he took offense. He threatened the thugs and, the next thing I knew, there was a family of gangsters in our joint courtyard with guns pointed at my neighbor. I heard the shouting and came out, only to behold this surreal moment. I quickly got the neighbors to put their guns away, convinced the new neighbor to go back into his house and dispelled the situation. But the gangster neighbors were now suspicious of me.

On Purim, I decided I was going to change that. I went to the gangster's house, somewhat drunk, dressed in the clown suit, with a fresh bottle of vodka, and asked them to make a *l'chaim* with me. They didn't want to drink, but that didn't stop me from giving all of them a hug, or kissing the Godfather of the gang on the forehead. That was at least ten years ago, and we're still friendly as a result. They make a barbeque a few times a year on the street and always invite us to eat with them.

That Purim ended with a lot of hugging and laughing. The next *Shabbos* came and I hugged the same friends that I had hugged on Purim without feeling any inhibitions at all. How strange, I thought to myself and I continued hugging people all year. I realized that something had changed on Purim. I had broken a barrier, and once it was broken it was gone forever. I had a feeling that this might be one of the secrets of Purim, but I wasn't sure. I had to test it out the next year.

I followed my new custom of drinking slower and drinking less. Once drunk, I headed to the house of the architect that had designed our house. We had some problems when we renovated our rundown home in Nachlaot. The contractors stole 70,000 NIS ($17,500), and then sued us for the rest of the construction that we wouldn't let them do since they stole the money.

We hired a lawyer and lost. We had to pay our lawyer, their lawyer, the legal fees and, of course, the judgment, which was around another 100,000 NIS ($25,000). The architect was a former friend of mine. I trusted him and we took the contractors he said he worked with all the time. From the time we called him to testify at the court case, he stopped speaking with me and would ignore me when he saw me on the street.

I decided that, since it was Purim and just about anything goes, I was going to head over to his house, say a *l'chaim* with him and try to make up. Today we're still not friends, but he did accept my apology. He was amazed to see me. I gave him a huge hug, drank a little vodka with him and told him, "What's in the past is in the past. We Jews have enough enemies." He laughed and we both moved on.

I started to realize that this is at least one of the secrets of Purim. You can have breakthroughs on Purim; personal and communal. It's not just a day of frivolity. It's a holy day for jumping forward like you can't on any other day of the year. Now that I had realized this, I started using Purim to my advantage. What else can I work on? I would ask myself, and then prepare for it the entire year.

One year I decided that I loved how Rabbi Shlomo Carlebach would call everyone "holy brother" and "holy sister." I thought I would love to, but I could never do that. Then came Purim. Everyone was "holy brother" and "holy sister," and, just like Purims past, once I broke down the barrier, it never went up again. Today, I have no problem calling anyone "holy brother" or "holy sister."

Then I decided to start working on deeper things. I actually don't remember what I worked on every year, because I would get drunk and then forget what happened. But whatever it was, I knew it would become part of who I am now, and it was always something good. The changes I made have become so much a part of me that I can't even remember what I used to be scared to do.

As the years passed, I thought more and more about Purim and what the Talmud said about it being a day higher than Yom Kippur. I would constantly ask myself how could Purim be higher than Yom Kippur? But I have adopted this trick of "act as if," or "fake it until you make it." So, I might not have understood what was so special about Purim, but I could acknowledge that it was and, when the day came, try to actually feel it. Eventually I got it. It took me almost twenty years of experimenting until I finally understood the secret of Purim.

TEMPORARY LAPSE OF INSANITY

When I was in high school, I fit in everywhere, but nowhere. Wherever I went in the high school social strata, I was accepted as an observer, but never a full time member. I had friends across the spectrum: friends that went to Harvard and became famous, others that became bestselling authors, but also those that had babies at sixteen or joined the Marine Corps because they didn't see any other opportunities. I wanted to go to the US Naval Academy or West Point so that I could have the best of both worlds: academia and adventure. The only problem was that I was such a poor student; so there was no chance I would get in.

I was the leader of the brass section in the marching band of an "integrated school" in South Florida. That meant we had a mix of every type of person South Florida had to offer, and that's a lot. The band was the integration of the integration. That was where it was easiest for me to go from group to group. None of my future Ivy League friends were in the marching band, but everyone else was there.

I had real conversations with several of the girls who got pregnant at sixteen. I was now eighteen, in my last year of high school, and had known these girls for a year or two. Marching band was intense. We had fifteen hours or more of practice a week. Then we performed together every Friday night for several months. We spent weekends together marching in the football field in the hot, Miami sun. It was a bonding experience. So when I spoke with these girls, they opened up to me. They trusted me.

I asked one girl, how could she possibly be pregnant at sixteen? Didn't she know about birth control? Even if the guy she was having relations with didn't use birth control, she could. She told me she *wanted* to have a baby because it made her "someone." It was a status symbol for her, "Like a purse with a Gucci logo on it," in her words. I could not believe it. She wanted to get pregnant and her other friends agreed with her. They told me, "She's going to be someone's mother. That's something." Then they turned it on me. "She's done something with her life. What have you done?" That came along with laughs, cheers, and some finger snaps.

My future Ivy League friends lived in my neighborhood and went to my synagogue. We were in the synagogue youth group together, in choir together and lived near each other; our parents were friends with each other. It was a middle-class neighborhood. I don't remember anyone with huge houses, flaunting their wealth, but no one was poor, at least not like some of the kids in the marching band.

I always thought my future Ivy League friends took themselves too seriously. They would "freak out" if an Advanced Placement class wasn't offered. Some of them had earned so many college credits they could finish college in a year. I'd ask them, "What's the point? Why rush? What are you so worried about: that you won't live to thirty and get to finish graduate school, or work for that corporation you always dreamt of?" But, these kids were driven.

The only time I was ever that driven was when I was trying to get to the last level of a video game. I admired their drive, although

I really believed it came at the expense of enjoying the view. It's like taking an airplane versus driving. I used to drive myself from Miami to New Jersey in university. It would take me two days and, although it was boring sometimes, it's one of the best memories I have. In their rush to finish three years of college in high school, what did my friends miss out on?

Then I had some really close friends in high school that joined the Marine Corps. They joined the Marines because it was perceived as the elite of the US military (advertising works). I still sing in my head, "Be all that you can be in the US Army." I even thought about joining the Army or the Marines as a regular grunt like everyone else. I knew my parents would freak out, but it seemed like an extension of the Boy Scouts.

I never joined the Marines. I was drafted into the Israeli Army after I became an Israeli citizen, but that was a bad joke, unfortunately. For one friend of mine, who was really a top notch person, the Marines helped her shine brighter. She was the head of the entire marching band and we were very close friends. She was black, grew up speaking Spanish at home, was beautiful, bright and full of life. I was astounded when she told me she was joining the Marine Corps, but her answer was pretty simple. "I can't afford college." The financial aid she was offered didn't cover enough. She could earn college credits and financial assistance for attending college if she joined the Marine Corps. It was a win-win for her and it worked out well.

I had another friend, a Jewish friend who lived a few houses away from me, who also joined the Marine Corps. He joined because he just didn't know what he wanted to do with his life. The Marine Corps shaped him up and gave him direction like none of us could believe. The Marines really turned a lost teenager into a man with a purpose. One of my other friends, who was working at Blockbuster Video at the time, was so impressed by our Marine buddy that he himself joined the Marine Corps the next year.

I kept in touch with these friends for a while, but eventually left the friendships behind. I met my two Marine friends a year later. The one who had joined out of high school was eventually stationed in Japan as a guard at the front gate of a Marine Corps base. The barrier at the gate hit him on the head by mistake once, and since then he blacked out randomly. He was discharged from the Marines and didn't know what he was going to do with his life.

If where people ended up after high school depended on their own self-perception, how did my self-perception affect me? I ended up living a life I could never have even dreamed of. For the most part, I've been blessed to live a life of little regret. Many times the decisions that affected the outcome of my life were as simple and scary as crossing a little line drawn on the road.

Eventually, I got myself into an Ivy League university for graduate school and did very well there. It took a lot of persistence and a little of the path less taken. Then I moved to Israel to study toward a PhD, then worked in hi tech, became self-employed and pursued my passions. My self-perception is still carrying me. It has influenced me to write this book and not just to dream of what could be, but to take the steps to get there.

Years ago, when I was in graduate school at the Hebrew University of Jerusalem, I had a professor who took me under his wing, both in and out of the university: Professor Yohanan Friedmann. He liked to make a lot of jokes but also had many wise things to say. A good friend of mine, a real genius, was rejected from the PhD program at Princeton where this professor had connections. Professor Friedmann, sure that he would be a shoo in, called the acceptance committee to ask what happened. Their answer: "A temporary lapse of insanity." They had already rejected my friend and accepted someone else. It was a done deal. My friend went to the University of Chicago instead and eventually became the head of the Islamic Studies department at a very prestigious American university.

Professor Friedmann told my friend and me over and over again, "It doesn't matter from which airport you take off, it's where you land that counts. He'll land in the right place." It doesn't matter where you grew up. It doesn't matter who you were in high school. It matters where you land. Maybe where you grew up affects your ability to see the possibilities of where you can land, but realize that it's all perception. It actually is a small world and a short life. Don't let self-perception hold you back.

MAKE THE MOST OF IT

When I was sixteen my Great Aunt Sally and her second husband Sol came to visit South Florida from Chicago. I got to know him a little better when I made a visit to Chicago on my spring break from university when I was twenty. By the time I made that visit to my relatives in Chicago, I had thought about my uncle Sol quite a bit because of the shocking advice he gave me back when I was sixteen.

We were in synagogue on *Shabbos* morning where I was very active, leading the services and participating as much as I could. I knew the secret passageways and was friendly with the custodian. Our synagogue was like a second home to me.

One *Shabbos*, sometime in the middle of the service, my uncle Sol took me by the shoulder, gently, and said nearly with tears in his eyes, "You have your whole life ahead of you. Make the most of it." That was it. He kissed me on the forehead and only four years later did we speak of it again.

I was hoping for some more words of wisdom. Since they didn't come, I asked my uncle if he remembered telling me at sixteen to "Make the most of my life," and he acknowledged that he remembered. "Why did you say that?"

"Because I thought it was the right thing to say at the time," was his answer.

Then I asked, "Did you make the most of your life?"

"Sometimes," my uncle said, "not always."

"How's it going for you?" he asked me. "I'm working on it," I said, "all the time."

"Good, my boy, good. That's what I wanted," and that was the end of the conversation. He died about a year later.

William Wallace, who fought for Scotland's freedom against the English, was tortured to death in 1305. He's quoted to have said, "Every man dies, but not every man really lives." I often ask myself, "Am I making the most of my life? Could I be doing more?"

I know when I die and my soul looks back at my life, all of the challenges I had in my lifetime will seem easy. I'll wonder why I stressed out about something that wasn't really so hard. But now it's hard and it's so hard that sometimes I forget to live. My uncle was saying to me, don't forget to live. Just like the boat that's pointed toward the horizon and doesn't know when or how it will get to its destination. As long as it stays on course, it will arrive.

IT IS A HARD AND ONEROUS TASK FOR THE ANGEL OF DEATH

In Israel, everyone has a friend named Shmuel. My friend Shmuel has had a hard life. He was married, but never had kids. Now he's divorced and, although he has many friends and even girlfriends, he feels like his life has no meaning. But Shmuel has a big problem. He's an optimist.

I understand Shmuel's problem because I have the same problem. You might feel depressed by your situation, but you know that one day, eventually, things will get better, or at least better than they are right now. So, even though Shmuel is a bit sad about his lot in life, he's a pretty happy guy. I've actually never heard him complain.

Not long ago, a very obese friend of mine ended up in the hospital after having a minor heart attack. His wife told me that he had company in the hospital because Shmuel was there too. I thought that was so nice of Shmuel to visit our mutual friend in the hospital and, when I told our friend's wife, she laughed. "Shmuel's not visiting my husband in the hospital. He's *in* the hospital." I didn't understand until she said, "Shmuel just had his fifth heart attack." I was stunned. "His fifth? I didn't even know he had his first!"

I made plans to visit both of them the next day, but they were both home by then. I saw Shmuel a few days later, eating a big fried meal and smoking a cigarette in-between bites. First I asked Shmuel how he was doing. "*Baruch Hashem.* I can't complain."

Then pointing to his meal he said, "I have good food, cigarettes and friends like you. Hashem has been so kind to me. Could I possibly ask for more?" I wished him good health and kept going.

What do you tell a guy who knows full well his situation but doesn't want to change it? A few weeks later I saw him again. He had clearly gained weight and was chain smoking. "Shmuel," I said, patting him on the back, "how are you doing?"

"*Baruch Hashem*. I can't complain."

I really had compassion for Shmuel and asked him as kindly as I could, "Are you really trying to kill yourself, Shmuel?" He went from smiling to a face that said, you too? Then he became defensive.

"No. If Hashem wants me to die, I'll die. For now I'm going to enjoy this cigarette," and he took a deep inhale of his partner in crime.

It's been two years since I learned of Shmuel's fifth heart attack. Recently I saw him on the street and asked him how he's doing. He told me he had another minor heart attack, but he was getting better. I wished him good health, gave him a hug and continued on my way. What else can you say to a man who doesn't want to take care of his health? I can understand Shmuel. His logic is, what am I living for? He's living, but not "living for." I have a wife and seven children, *Baruch Hashem*. I have a lot to live for. At least Shmuel didn't give up on living.

Rebbe Nachman is quoted as saying, "It is a hard and onerous task for the Angel of Death to kill everyone in the world all on his own. That is why he has helpers everywhere: the doctors to kill physically and the false leaders to kill spiritually." While I won't take Shmuel as my role model for health, I do take Shmuel as my role model for embracing life. Things might get better tomorrow and they might not, but at least learn from Shmuel how to enjoy the cigarette of life. Inhale deeply and let your exhale be a sweet fragrance that elevates all of those around you.

HIDDEN TRACK

Every morning I *daven* for around an hour and a half. I come to shul before the *minyan* and leave after everyone else has gone. My peace of mind fades quickly as I realize the stressful day that awaits me.

One morning I wrote something on the last page of my *siddur* to give me focus and direction. Here's the hidden track on this album.

Stay calm.
Trust in God.
Live boldly with purpose.

GLOSSARY

Aliyah, to go up.

Baruch Hashem, "blessed is God," thank God.

Bentching, praying.

Bima, raised section where the Torah is read.

Birkat hamazon, blessing after eating bread.

Chazzan, cantor.

Chevre, friends.

Daven, to pray.

Davening, prayers.

Dvar Torah, word of Torah.

Eruv, a rabbinical extension of a person's home so that Jews can carry objects on the Sabbath.

Etrog, citrus fruit used on Sukkot

Hashem, "the Name," meaning God.

Kaddish, prayer for the deceased.

kippah, see Yarmulke.

L'chaim, "to life".

Mincha, afternoon prayer.

Mitzvah, commandment from God.

Minyan, prayer quorum of ten Jewish men.

Motzei Shabbos, after the Sabbath has ended

Neshamah, soul.

Peyos, religious sidelocks.

Parnasah, livelihood.

Refuah shelaimah, full recovery.

Seder, order.

Shabbos or *Shabbat*, the Jewish Sabbath, from Friday night sunset to Saturday night sunset.

Shalom aleichem, peace unto you. The standard greeting between two religious Jews.

Sheitel, wig worn by religious Jewish women to keep their hair from being exposed.

Shofar, a ram's horn used as a musical instrument mainly on Rosh Hashanah (the Jewish New Year). It is a holy object used also for prayer.

Shuk, an open air marketplace for produce.

Shul, synagogue.

Shtender, the podium at the front of a shul, also a book stand.

Shtreimel, fur hat.

Siddur, prayer book.

Tallis or *tallit*, prayer shawl.

Tefillin, leather boxes containing scrolls of parchment inscribed with verses from the Torah.

Tzadik, righteous person.

Tzedakah, charity.

Tzitziot or tzitzis, strings and knots worn by Jewish men on four cornered garments. Even though most people don't wear four cornered garments, religious Jewish men wear a special garment so they can put tzitziot on it and fulfill the commandment.

Yarmulke or *kippah*, Jewish head cover for men.

WHY DID GOD CREATE US?

I have to first thank my wife, Noga, who always encourages me in my projects and in life in general. I'm very blessed to have her as my best friend and partner.

Noga suggested I let Vera Schwarcz read the book and Vera helped me at every level. She taught me how to make my stories more concise, come up with the chapter titles (most of which were her suggestions) and pushed me to finish the project. I can't thank Vera enough for her help.

Thank you to the other early readers of the book: Laura Milmeister, Zakai Ben-Chaim, Roni Isaiah, Michael Shalem, Noga Hullman, Reuven Prager, David Hendrie, Henry Valier and Sadie Lynn.

I have to give a special thanks to Sadie who went word by word improving my grammar and style. This is a much better book thanks to Sadie.

Thank you to Michael Avraham HaLevy. Several of the quotes in the book I learned from Michael Avraham. He was also my first reader. I'd send him the stories often an hour after writing them to get his feedback. It's thanks to his encouragement that I continued writing. Na Nach Nachma Nachman Meuman.

I want to thank my parents, Bonnie Bloom and Geoffrey Hullman, for caring so much about me and supporting me over the years. Thank you also to my brother, Jordan, for his support.

Thank you to my in-laws Professor Avram and Carmella Sidi for their support over the years. Also to my sister-in-law Yikrat for her support and for sharing her experience as a writer.

I want to thank two people specifically who changed my life for the better and without them I would have been telling different stories: Yoel Caroline and David Mitchell.

Thank you to Naftali Lowenstein who pushed me to finish this book after I decided not to run for Mayor of Jerusalem.

There were three freelance editors who worked on the manuscript. Thank you to each of them for their help: Maurice McBride, Patricia Vane and Richard Howard.

Thank you to my two teachers, rabbis, mentors and friends: Sholom Brodt and Shloime Gestetner.

Lastly, thank you God for making me a Jew.

Why did God create us? Because God loves stories.

MAY HIS LIGHT SHINE

A month before he died, my friend, mentor and teacher Sholom Brodt wrote me this poem after I showed him the cover of my book. I'm including it here in his memory.

> You'll figure it out when you get there
> journeys
> going arriving staying leaving
> moving forward backward
> sideways up down up
> higher
> circles spirals confusion clarity
> fear love awe
> sure unsure
> trusting sincere confident
> honest just generous
> grateful love friendship
> love jealous egoist
> dark lost disconnected
> falling standing jumping dancing
> alive open vulnerable
> it all doesn't make sense
> but you'll figure it out when you get there
> in the meantime sing dance
> learn celebrate b'simcha (with joy)
> (for Barak, may his light shine)

ABOUT THE AUTHOR

Barak Hullman is a storyteller, writer, entrepreneur and marketer. He moved to Jerusalem, Israel in 1995 to study for a PhD in Islamic studies where he met his wife, Noga. They have seven children. When Barak is not writing he's usually cooking, throwing pottery, singing, telling stories or planning his next project.

Website: barakhullman.com
Facebook: fb.me/barakauthor
Twitter: @barakhullman